HOW TO GET A GOOD JOB AND KEEP IT

Deborah Perlmutter Bloch, Ph.D.

VGM Career Horizons
a division of *NTC Publishing Group*
Lincolnwood, Illinois USA

Library of Congress Cataloging-in-Publication Data

Bloch, Deborah Perlmutter.
    How to get a good job and keep it / Deborah Perlmutter Bloch.
        p.   cm.
    Includes bibliographical references.
    ISBN 0-8442-4162-8
    1. Job hunting. 2. Employment interviewing. 3. Success in business. I. Title.
HF5382.7.B588 1992   92–23925
650.14—dc20   CIP

Published by VGM Career Horizons, a division of NTC Publishing Group.
© 1993 by NTC Publishing Group, 4255 West Touhy Avenue,
Lincolnwood (Chicago), Illinois 60646-1975 U.S.A.
Manufactured in the United States of America.

2 3 4 5 6 7 8 9 0 VP 9 8 7 6 5 4 3 2 1

About the Author

Deborah Perlmutter Bloch, Ph.D., is an associate professor of educational administration at Baruch College, the City University of New York. Previously, she worked as the director of MetroGuide, New York City's computer-based Career Information System; the coordinator of research for the Office of Occupational and Career Education of the New York City Board of Education; a high school guidance counselor; and an English teacher.

As a consultant, Dr. Bloch has worked with the National Career Information System at the University of Oregon, New York City's Job Center and the Dropout Prevention Program, and the Departments of Labor and Education of several states. She is currently involved in the development of career counseling courses for the University of Wollongong in Australia.

Dr. Bloch is past-president of the National Career Development Association and the Association of Computer-

Based Systems for Career Information. She remains active in these groups, as well as in the guidance division of the American Vocational Association.

She has published many articles in professional and popular magazines and given numerous presentations and workshops for counselors and teachers on how to help people with their career decisions and job searches.

Contents

Introduction: How This Book Can Help You

This book is for you if you are looking for, or thinking about looking for, your first full-time, paid job. Perhaps you are about to graduate from high school, a vocational program, or college. Maybe you are a homemaker who wants to earn money for your work. In any case, you are ready to move from the kind of work you have been doing to a different kind.

Wait a minute, you may be saying, if this is my first job, how can you be talking about the kind of work I have been doing? The answer is that you have been working all along, in school, at home, possibly in your community or religious organization, perhaps in neighborhood or volunteer activities. A good part of what you will learn in this book is how to use what you already know from this work to help you get and keep a good job.

How to Get A Good Job and Keep It is divided into three sections. The first section is about getting the job. The second section is about keeping that job, and what you can do on the first job to make it a successful experience. The third section is about moving on to your next job through promotion or change.

Section I   Section I, "Getting the Job," is made up of four chapters. Each of these chapters deals with a different step in the process of finding a job.

Chapter 1, "How to Get Started," helps you understand the habits of successful people, and provides a checklist of what you need to know to launch a successful job search.

Chapter 2, "Places—Where Are the Jobs?" helps you identify sources of jobs and ways of making contact with agencies and people that have the jobs that interest you. In case you are not certain what interests you, the chapter also provides some information about how to get help in identifying your career choices. It even gives you a brief interest inventory to help you begin.

Chapter 3, "Papers—Applications, Resumes, and More," gives you concrete information on what to expect in filling out applications and provides you with worksheets that you can use ahead of time to prepare for any application. Some jobs require a resume and a cover letter to mail with it. Tests are required for some jobs. Helpful hints for successful test taking are given. All of the papers and forms you may need in your job hunt are listed and explained.

Chapter 4, "People—Seven Steps to a Winning Interview," helps you through this crucial process, the one that ensures you get a job. In this chapter you learn what to expect during an interview and how to prepare yourself for it.

Section II   Section II, "Keeping Your Job," is about succeeding on the job and contains two chapters.

Chapter 5, "Hired!—Finding Out the Facts," gives you helpful hints on the kinds of information you want to find out from the company or organization that has hired you. The first part of the chapter deals with what you need to know before you accept a job offer. The second part helps with the first few days on the job. Having the right kinds of information will ensure that you and your boss or supervisor are operating on the same wavelength, that you have the same expectations about responsibilities and rewards, such as hours of work and paydays. You will learn how to fit in easily.

Chapter 6, "On-the-Job Success," is about the kinds of things you can do, and can avoid doing, on the job so that you are considered a valuable employee. Research has been done about what employers are looking for. This chapter lets you in on what employers have said about this. Through case studies, where you look at both the employee's and employer's points of view, you learn how to succeed. The chapter includes a checklist to help you organize your thinking.

Section III   Section III, "Career Changes," is about the future.

Chapter 7, "Moving Up," helps you build on the success of your first job to move up. There are suggestions for getting raises and promotions within your company.

Chapter 8, "Moving Out," provides tips on how to move to other organizations. The end of the chapter is about making your own opportunities and striking out on your own.

In all of the chapters, lots of worksheets and samples make this a practical book for your use. The book concludes with some additional sources of information.

This is the beginning of an exciting, productive period in your life. It is hoped that this book will help you get off to an informed and energetic start.

GETTING THE JOB

Section I

How to Get Started 1

When you opened this book, you made an important decision. You decided to take charge of your life—right now. Figuring out the kind of work you want to do and can do, and then going for that first successful full-time job, is a major step.

Our jobs influence not only how much money we have to spend, but also how we spend our time and, very often, where we spend our lives. In carrying out a successful job search, you will draw on many experiences you have had in other aspects of your life. That's good! You will probably also learn a great deal about yourself, what you like, and what makes you tick. That's good as well. Finally, in the very act of finding a job, you will probably develop new skills and attitudes that you will be able to draw on in other situations.

Develop the Habits of Success

Successful job seekers and job keepers often have the habits of people who are successful in many areas of life. One of the most interesting books recently written about success is called, *The 7 Habits of Highly Effective People.* The author, Steven R. Covey, urged readers to determine what they want, figure out their goals and aim for them, put the most important things first, *and* do all of this while recognizing their interdependence with others.

The most important part of job seeking is determining your occupational goal. To do this you must think about your own interests, skills, needs, and abilities, and take a realistic look at the jobs available in the area where you want to live and work. Of course, sometimes this may mean you will have to compromise. You may decide you are willing to move to get the kind of job you want. On the other hand, you may not be willing to move, but you may decide to continue your education. Sometimes, we take one job while we seek the education we need to get the job we would rather have.

Once you have determined your goal, you need to put first things first. It would be nice to have a magic wand that would move us from choosing an occupation to working at it. But there are many steps in between. These steps include finding out about employers who have openings in the job title that interest you, filling out various papers, and being interviewed. That's only the short list. Each of the activities I mentioned will probably consist of several steps in themselves. But if you keep your eye on your goal, your persistence will pay off in a job.

In preparing for the job interview, you will see the wisdom of Covey's suggestion that you must "seek first to understand, then to be understood." As you will learn in the chapter on interviewing, listening is often the key to a successful interview. And you must have a successful interview to be hired. Understanding others—your co-workers, your boss, and anyone who reports to you—is the key to job success at any level. There will be more about interpersonal relations in the second section of this book.

Perhaps the most important of the "seven habits" is being *proactive*. Being proactive means going out and doing things for yourself. Of course, that includes getting the help you need from appropriate sources, and this book will help you identify those. But it can also mean getting help from more than one person or agency if that's what it takes.

A recent television program showed discouraged young

men walking away from a factory. Each one had asked the first person they saw in the office, "Have you any job applications?" They were told "No," which was the truth. But, the employer said, "Why didn't they ask *when* applications *would* be available? Why didn't they ask for the manager's name so they could speak directly to her or him? Why didn't they show they cared about getting a job?" Now, it would be nice if that employer had been more concerned about others and had realized that inexperienced young people get nervous even asking for an application.

Yes, that employer could have been more helpful. But, once again, success comes down to helping yourself. If you are just trying to get your foot in the door, ask the same question many times in different ways. Ask for an application. Ask who has applications. Ask when applications will be available. Ask if applications are required. Remember all the no's still add up to only one no, but a single yes changes the picture entirely.

Learn the Skills of Job-seeking Success

Many people are concerned right now about you and your future. That's because leaders in business, government, and education recognize how important it is for each and every one of us to find the job we want. This is important both for personal satisfaction and the country's economy.

For these reasons, the National Occupational Information Coordinating Committee, a federal agency, developed "The National Career Development Guidelines." These guidelines were developed for organizations that provide education and training at the elementary school, middle or junior high school, high school and adult levels, to help counselors, teachers, and administrators plan their programs. Organized programs are helpful, but self-help works too. What follows is a set of eleven indicators from the "Guidelines" for high school students and adults. They are called indicators because mastery of certain skills indicates that you are ready to conduct a successful job search.

Use the checklist to measure your strengths and weaknesses. It will help you understand what you need to concentrate on when using this book. Come back to the checklist as you work through the first section to see for yourself all that you have learned.

READY TO FIND A JOB
A Checklist of Indicators

Directions: In the first column, place a check next to those job-seeking skills you think you have "NOW." Place a question mark next to the ones you would like to find out more about. If you are uncertain, leave the space blank. As you read through this book, come back and place a plus sign in the second column, "LATER," when you think you have really mastered a particular skill.

NOW   LATER   ESSENTIAL SKILLS FOR JOB
SEEKING

____   ____   1. Identify and appreciate personal interests, abilities, and skills

____   ____   2. Describe how skills developed in academic and vocational programs relate to career goals.

____   ____   3. Describe how educational achievements and life experiences relate to occupational opportunities.

____   ____   4. Identify individuals in selected occupations as possible information resources, role models, or mentors.

____   ____   5. Identify and use current career information resources, such as computerized career information systems and print materials.

____   ____   6. Describe career planning and placement services available through organizations, for example, schools and colleges, business and industry, labor and community agencies.

____   ____   7. Demonstrate skills to locate, interpret, and use information about job openings and opportunities.

   _____   _____   8. Demonstrate skills to establish a job-search network through colleagues, friends, and family.

   _____   _____   9. Demonstrate skills in preparing a resume and completing job applications.

   _____   _____   10. Demonstrate skills and behavior necessary for a successful job interview.

   _____   _____   11. Demonstrate skills to assess occupational opportunities, for example, working conditions, benefits, and opportunities for change.

Places—Where Are the Jobs?

You are ready to look for your first full-time, paid job. You have completed your education or training, or the part of it you plan to do now. Where do you go next? This chapter will help you identify the sources of jobs and how to use them. One of the most important things to remember in your job search is that you do not have to choose one method of searching or one agency to help you. You can use any or all of the ideas in this chapter so that you get the best possible job for you.

In the first part of the chapter you will find descriptions of various kinds of agencies that can help you in your job search. In the second part, you will learn how to use the newspaper and other advertisements and listings. Many people get jobs through people they know. The third section of this chapter helps you think about the people you know and how to get them to help you in your job search. The fourth part of this chapter is for those who may be uncertain about the kind of job they want. There is a short interest inventory and some suggestions of other places to get help in narrowing the choice of jobs. Finally, there is a set of guidelines to help you choose a career counselor if you decide you want some help in making a job selection or understanding how to carry out a job search.

Helpful Agencies

A school placement office is probably available to you if you are now attending a high school, college, or trade school. If you have previously attended a college, you may be able to use the services of the placement office, often for a fee, even if you are no longer enrolled. The counselors in the school placement or counseling office can provide a number of services. They can help you figure out the kind of job you want and are qualified for; they can help you improve your resume-writing and interviewing skills; and they can help you identify actual job openings. Some schools arrange for recruiters to meet with potential employees.

It is important to remember that there are two worlds of jobs. One is the world of business, from small one-person operations to giant multinational corporations. The other is the world of government. Jobs in government—at the local, state, or federal level—are called civil service jobs. They include almost every kind of occupation there is. The school placement office will often have lists of both business and civil service job openings.

State employment services also run employment offices located in many areas within each state. You can find these by looking under state listings in your local telephone directory. Some community or neighborhood organizations offer job placement assistance. You can find out about these by looking in local papers or on bulletin boards in libraries and other public places. These employment services will provide information about business job openings and civil service job listings.

Private employment agencies work for the employer who pays the fees. From your point of view, the agency is helping you find a job. From the employer's point of view, the agency is helping fill a vacant position. In most cases, this works out just fine. When you look at newspaper advertisements for jobs, you will see that many of them are placed by private employment agencies to which you can apply. You will also find listings of private employment agencies in your local classified telephone directory.

Private career counseling services help you assess your goals and develop resume-writing and interviewing skills, the kinds of skills presented in this book and others like it. However, many of these career counseling services do not provide job placement. The National Career Development Association, a professional organization of counselors, has prepared consumer guidelines for selecting a career counselor.

Personnel departments of large companies sometimes accept job applications on an ongoing basis. First, you need to figure out the kinds of companies that need the kind of work you do. It is pretty obvious that if you are looking for a job as a sales clerk, you can go to a department store, but the relationship between many jobs and industries is not always clear. In school placement offices and libraries, you can find career information in computer-based systems and in books such as the *Occupational Outlook Handbook*, which is published every two years by the United States Department of Labor's Bureau of Labor Statistics. In the description of the job that interests you, you will find descriptions of the industries in which that job is found. Knowledge of the industries can help you determine which companies in your area may need your work. If you need help understanding these connections, counselors and librarians can often provide it.

You can then identify the companies in your area on your own by asking a counselor or by looking in the classified yellow pages telephone directory. Be sure to read the section of this book on completing job applications. Then go to the company's personnel department and ask to complete an application.

Military recruitment offices fall into a unique category of employment agency, because taking a job in the military is different in many ways from taking a job in civilian employment. If you are considering the military as a first job, remember that there are different services that compete with each other, and the job of the recruiter is to get you to join the service he or she represents. One book about this, *Planning Your Military Career* by Robert McKay (VGM Career Horizons), describes recruiters as "persuasive individuals, who might be guilty of painting a more rosy picture of life in their services than actually awaits the enlistee." If you are thinking about a career or a job in the military, be sure to read this book or to get other reliable information.

Although all of these agencies can be helpful to you in your job search, there are differences of which you should be aware. The placement office in your school works for you. You are the customer whether the service is free or not. The school placement office counselors are interested in placing you in the best job they can.

Employment agencies, on the other hand, work for the companies with job vacancies. That is why you pay no placement fee. The fee is paid by the company. Their interest, therefore, is not in helping you but in finding the best possible person for the job. That does not mean that they will not be helpful to you. It does mean that you need to know their point of view.

State employment services are more neutral. Their goal is to make as many placements as possible so that fewer people are unemployed and the economy of the state is healthy. The range of services provided by the state employment service varies from state to state.

The private career counseling services work for you, the client, and you usually pay a fee. Some career counseling services will help you find a job, but most provide other services, so remember to look at the consumer guidelines at the end of this chapter if you want to get help from a career counselor.

Find the employment services most suited to your needs. Use them to identify job leads and to get any help offered in presenting yourself on a job. You need not stick to one choice. You can go to your school placement office, the state employment service, and register with several employment agencies. Before you sign any agreements with an employment service, be sure you know the following:

1. Is there a fee?

2. How much is the fee and who is responsible for it?

3. If you are paying, what is the agency promising to do?

Use the Employment Service Checklist that follows to identify and keep track of the services you are planning to use.

Employment Service Checklist

Check the types of services that are available and useful to you. Then fill in the actual names of the agencies and the information about them as you identify them.

Type	Name & Address	Fees	Services
___ School Placement Office	_____	___	_____
	_____		_____
	_____		_____
___ State Employment Service	_____	___	_____
	_____		_____
	_____		_____
___ Community Agency 1	_____	___	_____
	_____		_____
	_____		_____
___ Community Agency 2	_____	___	_____
	_____		_____
	_____		_____
___ Employment Agency 1	_____	___	_____
	_____		_____
	_____		_____
___ Employment Agency 2	_____	___	_____
	_____		_____
	_____		_____

___ Personnel Department 1   _____ ___ _____

                                      _____   _____

                                        _____   _____

___ Personnel Department 2   _____ ___ _____

                                        _____   _____

                                        _____   _____

___ Career Counselor   _____ ___ _____

                                        _____   _____

Advertisements and Listings

Answering an advertisement may lead to your first job. You can find job advertisements in your local newspaper in the classified section and often in specialized sections for business, education, and health. Several major newspapers, like the *New York Times* and the *Wall Street Journal,* carry ads for national companies. If you are interested in working for a large organization, you will want to check the ads in one or both of these while you are job hunting. You will also find ads in professional newspapers and magazines. Of course, these are jobs related to the interests of the readers. For example, *ComputerWorld* lists programmer and analyst jobs.

Some advertisements call for a written answer. To answer such an ad, you will need to prepare your resume and write a cover letter. Chapter 3 gives you help in resume preparation. Other advertisements ask that you call. You will find help in making telephone arrangements in chapter 4.

Newspaper advertisements are listed alphabetically by job title. However, some of these titles are not very specific. For example, there is often a large section listed as *college grad.* The first thing to do is to go through the newspaper for several days and write down *all* of the job titles that could be right for you. It is much better to apply for some jobs that are not appropriate than to miss the one that is right. Be sure to look most closely at the Sunday papers. Many more ads are usually found there.

Some job ads are placed directly by the employer, others by employment agencies. Employment agency ads usually list the name of the agency and contain some phrase like "fee paid" or "f/pd," which means that the employer pays the agency fee. Job advertisements are often written in a peculiar shorthand to save space and the money it costs. Here are two recent advertisements and their translations. After that, you will find a list of commonly used abbreviations and their meanings.

SAMPLE JOB ADVERTISEMENT 1
GAL/GUY FRIDAY
Acts rec, type 60wpm, gd telephone voice, computer & memory typewriter knldg helpful. Midtown loc. Call Gary btwn 10-4, 555-2378.

TRANSLATION OF JOB ADVERTISEMENT 1

A person who is able and willing to do a variety of office tasks is needed. The person will work on some bookkeeping with accounts receivable, must be able to type 60 words per minute, and must be able to speak clearly on the telephone. It would be helpful if he or she also knows how to use a computer or memory typewriter. The job is located in the midtown area. If you are interested, call the number given between 10 in the morning and 4 in the afternoon and ask for Gary. [This ad was placed by the company itself. No starting salary is mentioned.]

SAMPLE JOB ADVERTISEMENT 2
College Grad   f/pd   14–16K
Prestig cos have several entry level openings for indivs w/interest in pr/advtg. Candidate should be articulate and possess interpersonal skills. Typg reqd. WP a +, gd benefits, tuition. Call Mr. Horton, 555-8787.

TRANSLATION OF JOB ADVERTISEMENT 2

This ad was placed by an employment agency and groups several jobs that the agency is trying to fill. Although the jobs are for college graduates with an interest in public relations and advertising, the employee will be working, at least part of the time, as a typist. In fact, knowledge of word processing is a plus, or a help in getting the job. The jobs are with well-known companies and have good benefits, usually health insurance and paid vacation, in addition to the salary. Tuition will be paid for additional education. This usually means for education related to the job functions.

List of advertisement abbreviations

Following is a list of commonly used abbreviations and their meanings. However, there really is no complete list. The best trick is to try reading the ad aloud, filling in letters to make all the abbreviated words complete.

Abbreviation	Translation
a+	a plus (if you have this, you are a better candidate)
acctg	accounting
advc	advancement
agcy	agency
appt	appointment
asst	assistant
begnr	beginner
bkpg	bookkeeping
bnfts	benefits
clk	clerk
co	company (mjr co means major company)
col grad	college graduate
dept	department
dict	dictation
EOE	Equal Opportunity Employer
eves	evenings
exp nec	experience necessary
exp pfd	experience preferred
f/pd	fee paid
f/t	full-time
gd	good
immed	immediate or immediately
inq	inquire
k	thousands (usually annual salary in dollars)
loc	location or located
mfg	manufacturing
mgmt	management
ovtm	overtime (sometimes written o/t)
opty	opportunity
ofc	office
pd vac	paid vacation

p/t	part-time
refs	references
secty	secretary
sr	senior (usually means experienced)
w/	with (w/wo means with or without)
wkend	weekend
wpm	words per minute
yr	year

Civil service announcements are another source of information about jobs. These listings appear separately for city or county, state, and federal jobs. You can usually find the lists in school placement offices, state employment service offices, and libraries. Since many civil service jobs require tests to prove that you can do the job, an announcement is often of a test rather than of a job itself. If you are interested in the job and believe you are qualified, do not let the idea of a test keep you from applying. Suggestions for preparing for civil service tests will be given in the next chapter.

A typical announcement begins with a list of jobs that are open or of examinations that you can apply for. Many of the jobs that are listed will be of no interest to you. However, you need to find only the one that is right for you. After the list, each job will be fully described, usually on following pages. The announcement of each job will usually contain a description of the position, the qualifications needed to apply, and the way that selection will be made. It will also contain a statement of what to do next if you are interested. Often you must send for an application form for the job or for the examination.

If you cannot get to any of the kinds of agencies mentioned to see the lists, you can write to the employment service of your state for state jobs. For federal jobs, you can write to the U. S. Office of Personnel Management, using the address in your local telephone directory. For jobs with the United States Postal Service, you can get examination applications at your local post office.

It is very important that you follow the directions for all civil service job and examination applications carefully. Since civil service jobs are governed by laws to protect all applicants equally, deadlines are deadlines!

A copy of an announcement from the New York State Department of Civil Service for a test for an electrocardiograph technician is reproduced on the following two pages. Notice that you could apply for this test without experience if you had completed a course in using the

EKG machine. Notice that you must pick up an application for the examination in person and then mail it. Many places are listed to pick one up. Finally, notice that you must send a $5.00 fee with your application and that your application must be filed no later than a particular date.

NEW YORK STATE ANNOUNCES
OPPORTUNITIES IN GOVERNMENT

NO. 26-667

ELECTROCARDIOGRAPH TECHNICIAN

$15,709*

*Beginning Salary Effective 4-1-87

THE POSITION: Electrocardiograph Technicians are employed in New York State government with the Department of Health, the Office of Mental Health, the Office of Mental Retardation and Developmental Disabilities, and the State University System. At present, there are three vacancies in Stony Brook and one in each of the following locations: Kings Park, Rochester, Thiels and Syracuse.

As an <u>Electrocardiograph Technician</u>, under professional direction, you would operate electrocardiograph (EKG) machines in administering tests to record the action of a patient's heart muscle for the diagnosis of heart ailments by a physician. You would also be responsible for performing minor maintenance and adjustments on the equipment; keeping and ordering required supplies; and performing clerical tasks in relation to the electrocardiograph program.

MINIMUM QUALIFICATIONS: As of the date of the written test, you must meet one of the following requirements:

Either I. six months of full-time paid experience in the operation of an EKG machine;

Or II. successful completion of a course in the operation of an EKG machine.

Note: If you qualify under "II," you must submit, with your application, evidence of successful completion of the course in operating an EKG machine.

SELECTION: There will be a <u>written test</u> which you must pass in order to be considered for appointment. The written test will be designed to test for knowledge, skills, and/or abilities in such areas as:

1. Anatomy and terminology related to electrocardiography
2. Operation and maintenance of an electrocardiograph machine
3. Techniques involved in taking electrocardiographs

Written Test To Be Held JANUARY 24, 19 -
Applications MUST Be Postmarked No Later Than DECEMBER 22, 19
A $5 Application Fee Must Accompany Your Application

SB-1/TB-2 RJP-d1   SEE REVERSE SIDE

NO. 26-667 ELECTROCARDIOGRAPH TECHNICIAN G-8

XD-17.1 (9/76)   **New York State - An Equal Opportunity Employer**

INFORMATION FOR CANDIDATES

APPLICATION FORMS: You may obtain forms at the following offices of the State Department of Civil Service: The W. Averell Harriman NYS Office Building Campus, Albany, NY 12239; 55th Floor, Two World Trade Center, New York, NY 10047; 6th Floor, The Adam Clayton Powell State Office Building, 163 West 125th Street, New York, NY 10027; or Room 303, 65 Court Street, Buffalo, NY 14202. Applications may also be obtained by calling in person at one of the local offices of the NYS Employment Service; these offices cannot handle mail requests. Specify examination number and title. Mail your application when completed to the Department of Civil Service, The W. Averell Harriman NYS Office Building Campus, Albany, NY 12239. The Department of Civil Service reserves the right to reject for lateness or to accept applications filed after the advertised filing period. All statements made on your application are subject to investigation and a medical examination may be required.

New York State Residence Not Required

ADMISSION TO EXAMINATION: Notice to appear for the test will be conditional as review of applications may not be made until after the first test. If you have not received your notice to appear within three days of the date of the written test, call (518) 457-5483 if taking the test in Albany; (518) 457-7020 for New York City Test Center; (518) 457-7022 or 457-7021 for all other Test Centers.

In accordance with State Law, Governor's Executive Order 6, and Section 504 of the Federal Rehabilitation Act of 1973, as amended, the State of New York does not discriminate against handicapped persons. It is the policy of the NYS Department of Civil Service to provide for and promote the equal opportunity of employment, compensation and other terms and conditions of employment without discrimination because of age, race, creed, color, national origin, sex, sexual orientation, disability or marital status.

This announcement is being issued and the examination will be held in compliance with the New York State Civil Service Law and the Rules and Regulations of the New York State Department of Civil Service.

TEST ARRANGEMENTS: Saturday Religious Observers - Handicapped Persons: If special arrangements for testing are required, indicate this on your application form.

Note: Fingerprints are sometimes required at the time of appointment. When they are required, the fee involved must be paid by the appointee.

APPLICATION FEE: A fee of $5.00 is required for each separately-numbered examination for which you apply. The required fee *must* accompany your application. Send check or money order payable to the NYS Department of Civil Service and write the examination number(s) and your social security number on your check or money order. *Do not send cash. As no refunds will be made,* you are urged to compare your qualifications carefully with the requirements for admission and file only for those examinations for which you are clearly qualified. An exception to the fee requirement will be made only for persons receiving Supplemental Social Security payments or public assistance (Home Relief or Aid to Dependent Children), provided Foster Care, or certified Job Training Partnership Act eligible through a state or local social service agency, and for those who are unemployed and primarily responsible for the support of a household. Individuals wishing to claim this waiver of fee on the basis of Supplemental Social Security, Home Relief or Aid to Dependent Children, must certify on their application that they are receiving public assistance and indicate the type of assistance they are receiving, the agency providing the assistance and their case number. Persons claiming this waiver through the Foster Care or Job Training Partnership Act Certification must specify the program and name of their contact agency. Such claims are subject to later verification and, if not supported by appropriate documentation, are grounds for barring appointment.

Pursuant to collectively-negotiated agreements between the State of New York and the Civil Service Employees Association, Inc., State employees in the Administrative Services, Institutional Services, or Operational Services negotiating units at the time of application for an examination are not obligated to submit any examination fee with their application. Such eligible employees must print "CSEA - No Fee" on the application form.

Getting Help from People You Know

Networking is a popular term that gives a technical sound to a technique that people have been using for a very long time. Basically, it means that you tell all the people you know that you are looking for a job and ask them to help you. Do not think that you do not know anybody who can help you. Think of the word *network*. Picture a *network*. It is not a single string from you to one person and another from you to another person. It is like a web with strings from you to the people you know and from them to the people they know. People generally like to help others. One reason is because it makes them feel good. The other is because it increases their own network of people they know.

The first thing to do is to make a list of everyone you know. Consider people from all aspects of your life: family; friends; parents or children of friends; teachers; fellow members of religious, professional, and community organizations; and sports teammates or opponents.

The next step is to think of what you want from each of these people. How can each one help you? Some may actually be employed by or run organizations in which you would like to work. Others may know people in the kinds of organizations you would like to work for. Still others may be just a shot in the dark. That is, you can't think of how they can help you, but it's worth seeing if they can. Your approach to each person may have to be a little different. You will be able to speak directly to some people when you see them in the course of everyday affairs. You may need to telephone or write others.

Try to be as direct and specific as you can in your approach. Say something like, "I am graduating from community college with a degree in office management. I will be ready to start work the first of February. If you can think of anywhere I might apply or anyone I should speak to, I would appreciate it."

If that's not like your situation at all, say something like, "I am graduating from high school, and I will be looking for a job where I can do a lot of outdoor work. I really don't mind moving around and lifting heavy things. You know, I've done a lot of that around the house for the last few years. If you can think of any openings I might apply for or anyone I should speak to, please let me know."

Maybe that still doesn't sound right for you. You may want to try something like, "I'm looking for a job in sales where I can use some of those persuasive skills I have learned in all those volunteer fundraisers for the community center. Do you know anyone looking for a mature, skilled salesperson? I would really appreciate any leads you could give me."

One of the most important techniques for a job search is keeping records of what you have done and where it has led. This is particularly important in networking, since one contact may lead to another. Here is an example of the kind of record you could keep for networking:

Networking Records

SAMPLE: Name <u>Lois Rich</u>

Address <u>Ferry Road, Bristol, RI</u>

Telephone <u>(401) 555-2664 (work)</u>

Source of Contact <u>Friend of Uncle Paul</u>

Method of Contact <u>I telephoned her at work.</u>

Date(s) of Contact <u>2/17</u>

Results/Follow-up <u>She asked me to send her a resume.</u>

<u>Sent 2/19. Call her 2/28.</u>

CONTACT 1: Name _____

Address _____

Telephone _____

Source of Contact _____

Method of Contact _____

Date(s) of Contact _____

Results/Follow-up _____

_____

_____

CONTACT 2: Name _____

Address _____

Telephone _____

Source of Contact _____

Method of Contact _____

Date(s) of Contact _____

Results/Follow-up _____

_____

_____

CONTACT 3: Name _____

Address _____

Telephone _____

Source of Contact _____

Method of Contact _____

Date(s) of Contact _____

Results/Follow-up _____

_____

_____

CONTACT 4:   Name _____
Address _____
Telephone _____
Source of Contact _____
Method of Contact _____
Date(s) of Contact _____
Results/Follow-up _____
_____
_____

CONTACT 5:   Name _____
Address _____
Telephone _____
Source of Contact _____
Method of Contact _____
Date(s) of Contact _____
Results/Follow-up _____
_____
_____

CONTACT 6:   Name _____
Address _____
Telephone _____
Source of Contact _____
Method of Contact _____
Date(s) of Contact _____
Results/Follow-up _____
_____
_____

CONTACT 7:   Name _____
Address _____
Telephone _____
Source of Contact _____
Method of Contact _____
Date(s) of Contact _____
Results/Follow-up _____
_____
_____

Choosing an Occupation

Some people looking for their first job know what they want to do. Others are not as certain. If you have graduated from high school and you have not taken particular courses in a business or vocational area, or if you are graduating from college with a major in a liberal arts or science discipline, you may need some help in making a career choice. Even if you have studied a subject that leads to a particular occupation, that may not be the occupation that now interests you.

Few people choose an occupation and stick to it for life. It has been estimated that most people make three to four career changes in their lives; that's not just job changes, but changes in direction. If you are in the position of making a choice at this time, there are a number of sources of help for you.

At the beginning of this chapter, several types of agencies that provide job placement assistance were identified. A number of these also provide help with choosing a career. If you are still in high school or college, there is almost certainly a counseling office to help you. That is a good place to begin. Some state employment services also offer testing. Sometimes this is available only to certain groups, such as those between 16 and 21 years of age, or those who are starting to work after being homemakers. Your local telephone directory will lead you to your state employment service.

In addition, some community agencies and universities offer career counseling. You can find out about these through local libraries, from your clergyman, or by contacting a state university directly. The private career counseling services mentioned earlier may prove helpful. Be sure to ascertain the qualifications of the counselors in any private service, using the consumer guidelines at the end of this chapter.

Some people prefer to work through the process of career decision making on their own. If you would like to do that, there are some things you can do. Your local library or community college may provide access to a computer-based career information delivery system. These systems help you develop a list of careers that meet your interests, needs, and abilities. The systems then provide information on the careers, their entry-level requirements, the opportunities for advancement, and the industries in which they are most often found. Some systems will even provide information on specific employers in your state or region of the state.

At the end of this section, you will find a set of questions and answers—The Skills Assessment Questionnaire, adapted from Quest, the exploratory part of the Career Information System. The Career Information System is in use in sixteen states, so you may be able to find it at your school or library. You can take The Skills Assessment Questionnaire and see what occupations it suggests for you. You can then use the Career Information System, or another computer-based career information delivery system, to get information on the occupations or to continue your self-assessment.

If you do not have access to a Career Information System, your counselor or librarian can help you get more information about any occupations that interest you. There are a number of books that can help you in this process. The *Occupational Outlook Handbook* provides excellent brief descriptions of jobs. If you want to read more about a particular occupation or industry, look for books like *Opportunities in High Tech Careers* or *Opportunities in Insurance Careers,* both published by VGM Career Horizons. There are hundreds of books about individual careers. *What Color is Your Parachute?* by Richard Nelson Bolles (Ten Speed Press) gives techniques for career choosing that have been used successfully by many people. Another book you might find helpful is *How to Choose the Right Career* by Louise Welsh Schrank (VGM Career Horizons).

Remember, The Skills Assessment Questionnaire is just a way to get started thinking about your first job choice if you haven't already done so. It contains only about one hundred occupations, while the Career Information System contains over three hundred. For example, all of the careers requiring graduate study for a first job, such as lawyers and doctors, have been left out of the Skills Assessment Questionnaire. This version is not really designed for long-range planning. It is to help you identify some first job choices that require, at most, a four-year college degree.

The Skills Assessment Questionnaire

The Skills Assessment Questionnaire* that follows consists of 16 items. Think about each skill, and decide whether this is a skill you possess and if you would like to use it on a job. For example, the first skill listed deals with the ability to do continuous work. Decide if you are able to do continuous work; ask yourself if you want to. If the answer to both questions is *yes*, mark Item 1 "yes." If you cannot do continuous work, or prefer not to, mark Item 1 "no."

After you answer the 16 questions, turn to the JOB MATCHING SECTION, which immediately follows. Fill in the circles at the top of the first page to match your "yes" answers to the sixteen questions. This is your skills profile. The skills profile for each job has already been filled in. Go down the pages, job by job, and note the number of matches between your skills profile and each job's. You will then be able to see which jobs match your strengths and interests.

1. *Continuous:*
   On some jobs you do the same things many times a day and you work at a steady pace. Is this type of work for you? _____ YES   _____ NO

2. *Precise:*
   On some jobs there is little room for error so you must be very exact in your work. Is this type of work for you? _____ YES   _____ NO

3. *Using Facts:*
   On some jobs you use factual information to decide what to do. Is this type of work for you? _____ YES   _____ NO

4. *Working with Others:*
   On some jobs you must deal with many different people to get your work done. Is this type of work for you? _____ YES   _____ NO

5. *Persuading:*
   On some jobs you talk with people to try to influence other people's actions or ideas. Is this type of work for you? _____ YES   _____ NO

6. *Decision Making:*
   On some jobs you are responsible for making major decisions about projects, plans, and other people's duties. Is this type of work for you? _____ YES   _____ NO

7. *Change*
   On some jobs you must move often from one task to another and use several different skills. Is this type of work for you? _____ YES   _____ NO

---

*The Skills Assessment Questionnaire is an adaptation of QUEST, copyrighted by the National Career Information System, University of Oregon, 1987, and is used with their permission.

8. *Creative:*
On some jobs you must express feelings and ideas in artistic ways. Is this type of work for you? _____ YES   _____ NO

9. *Eye-Hand Coordination:*
On some jobs you need to be very good at handling objects quickly as you see them. Is this type of work for you? _____ YES   _____ NO

10. *Working with Fingers:*
On some jobs you need to be able to do very precise work with your fingers. You need to work with small things very quickly and carefully. Is this type of work for you?
_____ YES   _____ NO

11. *Checking Accuracy:*
On some jobs you need to be very accurate at reading or copying written materials. You have to be very good at things like proofreading numbers and words. Is this type of work for you?
_____ YES   _____ NO

12. *Use of Words:*
On some jobs you need to be able to read and understand instructions easily. You have to express yourself very clearly in writing, or when talking with people. Is this type of job for you?
_____ YES   _____ NO

13. *Use of Numbers:*
On some jobs you need to be able to work very quickly and accurately with numbers or measurements. Is this type of work for you? _____ YES   _____ NO

14. *Catching on to Things:*
On some jobs you need the ability to understand procedures and the reasonings behind them. You have to be very good at figuring out complicated things quickly and easily. Is this type of work for you? _____ YES   _____ NO

15. *Seeing Detail:*
On some jobs you need to be able to tell slight differences in shapes of objects and lengths of lines. You have to be able to see detail in objects, pictures, or drawings. Is this type of work for you? _____ YES   _____ NO

16. *Physical Activity:*
Jobs require different amounts of physical activity. On some jobs you need to be very active, often handling 25-pound objects and sometimes more. Is this type of work for you?
_____ YES   _____ NO

Job Matching Section

Your Skills Profile:

Column key:
1. CONTINUOUS
2. PRECISE
3. USING FACTS
4. WORKING WITH OTHERS
5. PERSUADING
6. DECISION MAKING
7. CHANGE
8. CREATIVE
9. EYE-HAND COORDINATION
10. WORKING WITH FINGERS
11. CHECKING ACCURACY
12. USE OF WORDS
13. USE OF NUMBERS
14. CATCHING ON TO THINGS
15. SEEING DETAIL
16. PHYSICAL ACTIVITY

(First column = NUMBER OF MATCHES)

• JOB TITLES •	✓	1	2	3	4	5	6	7	8	9	10	11	12	13	14	15	16
Accountants & Auditors			•	•			•					•	•	•	•		
Animal Caretakers								•		•	•		•		•		•
Air Traffic Controllers			•				•	•				•	•	•	•	•	
Bakers			•							•	•				•	•	•
Bank Tellers		•	•		•					•	•	•	•	•	•	•	
Bartenders					•								•	•			
Body & Fender Repairers			•	•			•			•	•		•	•	•	•	•
Bookkeepers			•							•	•		•	•	•	•	
Building Maintenance Workers			•				•			•	•		•	•	•	•	•
Bus & Taxi Drivers				•	•					•			•		•		•
Buyers					•	•	•	•					•	•	•		
Carpenters			•	•			•			•	•		•	•	•	•	•
Cashiers		•	•		•					•	•	•	•	•	•		
Cement Masons			•	•						•					•	•	•
Chefs & Cooks			•					•		•		•	•		•		
Child Care Workers					•			•					•		•		•
Claims Adjusters & Examiners			•	•								•	•	•	•		
Coal & Mineral Mining Occupations		•	•							•					•		
Commercial Artists									•	•	•	•	•	•	•	•	•
Commercial Fishers		•															•
Computer Operators			•					•		•	•	•	•	•	•	•	
Computer Programmers			•	•								•	•	•	•	•	
Construction Laborers		•	•														•
Data Entry Operators		•	•							•	•	•	•		•	•	
Dental Hygienists			•		•					•	•		•	•			
Designers, Clothes			•	•						•	•	•	•	•	•	•	
Designers, Floral					•			•	•	•	•	•	•	•	•		
Designers, Interior					•	•	•		•	•	•	•	•	•	•	•	
Drafters			•	•						•	•	•	•	•	•	•	

	NUMBER OF MATCHES	CONTINUOUS	PRECISE	USING FACTS	WORKING WITH OTHERS	PERSUADING	DECISION MAKING	CHANGE	CREATIVE	EYE-HAND COORDINATION	WORKING WITH FINGERS	CHECKING ACCURACY	USE OF WORDS	USE OF NUMBERS	CATCHING ON TO THINGS	SEEING DETAIL	PHYSICAL ACTIVITY
Electricians		•	•				•		•	•		•	•	•	•	•	•
Electronics Assemblers	•	•	•						•	•						•	
Engineers		•	•			•	•		•	•	•	•	•	•	•		
Farmers & Ranchhands			•			•	•		•			•	•	•	•	•	
Firefighters							•		•			•		•			•
Foresters			•	•		•	•					•	•	•	•		
Freight Handlers	•								•								•
General Office Clerks		•								•	•	•	•	•	•		
Groundskeepers & Gardeners		•															•
Hair Stylists				•			•		•	•		•			•	•	
Handcrafters		•					•	•	•			•		•	•		
Health & Safety Inspectors		•	•	•								•	•	•	•		
Heavy Equipment Operators		•							•	•				•	•	•	•
Hotel Desk Clerks				•			•		•	•	•	•	•				
Interpreters & Translators		•	•							•	•		•				
Jewelers		•	•				•		•	•		•	•	•	•		
Laundry & Dry Cleaning Workers		•															•
Law Enforcement Officers				•			•		•		•	•		•	•	•	
Legal Assistants		•	•	•			•				•	•	•	•			
Library Assistants				•			•		•	•	•	•		•	•	•	•
Machinists		•	•				•		•	•		•	•	•	•	•	•
Meat Cutters		•	•						•	•				•	•	•	•
Mechanics, Automobile		•	•				•		•	•		•		•	•	•	•
Mechanics, Heavy Equipment		•	•				•		•	•		•	•	•	•	•	•
Medical Laboratory Workers		•	•				•		•	•		•	•	•	•		
Messengers	•			•													
Metal Refining Occupations	•	•															•
Nurses Aides & Orderlies				•			•										•
Nurses (LPN)		•		•			•		•	•		•			•	•	•
Nurses (RN)		•	•	•					•	•	•	•	•	•	•	•	
Office Machine Repairers		•	•				•		•	•		•	•	•	•	•	•
Packers & Wrappers	•								•	•							•
Painters & Paperhangers		•							•	•		•	•	•	•	•	•
Performing Artists									•	•	•		•	•	•	•	•

Occupation	NUMBER OF MATCHES	CONTINUOUS	PRECISE	USING FACTS	WORKING WITH OTHERS	PERSUADING	DECISION MAKING	CHANGE	CREATIVE	EYE-HAND COORDINATION	WORKING WITH FINGERS	CHECKING ACCURACY	USE OF WORDS	USE OF NUMBERS	CATCHING ON TO THINGS	SEEING DETAIL	PHYSICAL ACTIVITY
Personnel Officers			•	•		•					•	•	•	•			
Petroleum Processing Occupations		•	•								•	•	•				
Photographers		•		•				•	•	•	•	•	•	•			
Plumbers & Pipefitters		•	•				•		•	•	•	•	•	•		•	•
Printing Production Occupations		•	•				•		•	•	•	•	•	•			
Production Assemblers	•	•							•	•				•			
Public Relations Workers				•	•	•	•				•	•	•	•	•		
Pulp & Paper Workers		•	•						•		•	•	•				
Railroad Conductors		•	•		•	•					•	•		•			
Recreation Attendants			•								•	•	•	•			
Salespeople				•	•				•		•	•	•	•			
Secretaries		•		•			•		•	•	•	•	•	•	•		
Security Guards	•			•										•			
Service Station Attendants				•			•					•	•	•	•	•	
Shipping & Receiving Clerks		•	•				•			•	•	•	•	•			
Shoe Repairers		•	•						•	•	•		•	•			
Social Service Aides				•			•				•	•	•	•			
Social Workers				•	•	•					•	•	•				
Surveyor Helpers	•	•															•
Teacher Aides				•			•			•	•	•	•				
Teachers				•	•	•	•				•	•	•	•	•		
Technicians, Broadcast		•	•						•	•	•	•	•	•			
Technicians, Computer Maintenance		•	•	•		•	•		•	•	•	•	•	•			
Technicians, Dental Laboratory		•	•				•		•	•	•	•	•	•			
Technicians, Emergency Medical			•	•					•	•	•	•	•	•	•	•	
Technicians, Engineering		•	•						•	•	•	•	•	•	•		
Technicians, Fish & Wildlife			•				•		•	•		•		•			
Technicians, Health		•	•	•					•	•	•	•	•	•	•		
Technicians, Nuclear Power		•	•				•		•	•	•	•	•	•		•	
Technicians, Solar		•	•				•		•	•	•	•	•	•		•	
Telephone & Teletype Operators		•		•					•	•	•	•		•			
Telephone Installers & Repairers		•	•	•			•		•	•	•	•	•	•			
Textile Machine Operators	•	•															•
Therapists, Physical			•	•	•	•			•	•	•	•	•	•	•		

	NUMBER OF MATCHES	CONTINUOUS	PRECISE	USING FACTS	WORKING WITH OTHERS	PERSUADING	DECISION MAKING	CHANGE	CREATIVE	EYE-HAND COORDINATION	WORKING WITH FINGERS	CHECKING ACCURACY	USE OF WORDS	USE OF NUMBERS	CATCHING ON TO THINGS	SEEING DETAIL	PHYSICAL ACTIVITY
Travel Agents					●	●						●	●	●	●		
Truck Drivers		●								●		●			●	●	●
Upholsterers			●	●						●	●	●	●		●	●	●
Waiters & Waitresses					●							●		●			
Welders			●	●						●	●		●		●	●	●
Woodworking Machine Operators		●	●							●					●	●	●
Word Processors & Typists			●							●	●	●	●	●	●	●	
Writers & Editors				●	●				●	●		●	●	●	●	●	

Guidelines for Selecting a Career Counselor

Sometimes it seems that virtually everyone is a vocational coach, ready and eager to give advice, suggestions, and directions. Unfortunately, all are not equally able to provide the kind of help people need in making decisions about what to do with their lives. Promises and luxurious trappings are poor substitutes for competency. Thus, the selection of a professional career counselor is a very important task. The following guidelines are offered to assist you in making the selection.

Credentials of the professional career counselor

A Nationally Certified Career Counselor is a counselor who has achieved the highest certification in the profession. Further, it means that the career counselor has

- earned a graduate degree in counseling or in a related professional field from a regionally accredited higher education institution.

- completed supervised counseling experience which included career counseling.

- acquired a minimum of three years of full-time career development work experience.

- obtained written endorsements of competence in career counseling from a work supervisor and a professional colleague.

- successfully completed a knowledge-based certification examination.

Other professional counselors may be trained in one- or two-year counselor preparation programs with specialties in career counseling, and may be licensed or certified by national or state professional associations.

What do career counselors do?

The services of career counselors differ, depending on competence. A professional or Nationally Certified Career Counselor helps people make decisions and plans related to life/career directions. The strategies and techniques are tailored to the specific needs of the person seeking help.

It is likely that the career counselor will do one or more of the following:

- conduct individual and group personal counseling sessions to help clarify life/career goals.

- administer and interpret tests and inventories to assess abilities, interests, etc., and to identify career options.

- encourage exploratory activities through assignments and planning experiences.

- utilize career planning systems and occupational information systems to help individuals better understand the world of work.

- provide opportunities for improving decision-making skills.

- assist in developing individualized career plans.

- teach job-hunting strategies and skills, and assist in the development of resumes.

- help resolve potential personal conflicts on the job through practice in human relations skills.

- assist in understanding the integration of work and other life roles.

- provide support for persons experiencing job stress, job loss or career transition.

Ask for a detailed explanation of services provided (such as career counseling, testing, employment search strategy planning and resume writing). Make sure you understand the service, and your degree of involvement and financial commitment.

Fees   Select a counselor who is professionally trained and will let you choose the services you desire. Make certain you can terminate the services at any time, paying only for services rendered.

Promises   Be skeptical of services that make promises of more money, better jobs, resumes that get speedy results or an immediate solution to career problems.

Ethical practices   A professional or Nationally Certified Career Counselor is expected to follow the ethical guidelines of such organizations as The National Career Development Association, The American Association for Counseling and Development, and The American Psychological Association. Professional codes of ethics advise against grandiose guarantees and promises, exorbitant fees, and breaches of confidentiality, among other things. You may wish to ask for a detailed explanation of services offered, your expected financial and time commitments, and a copy of the ethical guidelines used by the career counselor you are considering.

These guidelines were produced by the National Career Development Association and are reprinted with their permission.

Summary Worksheet

In this chapter, you have examined the sources of jobs and information about jobs. Use this summary worksheet to be sure you have left no stone unturned in your job search.

_____ I have identified agencies that can help me in my job search. They are: _____

_____

_____

_____ I have thought about companies I can apply to directly. They are: _____

_____

_____

_____ I know the headings in newspapers under which I can look for jobs that interest me. They include: _____

_____

_____

_____ I know how to read newspaper advertisements.

_____ I know where to find civil service job announcements.

_____ I have identified some people I know who can help me. They are: _____

_____

_____ I know what job I am seeking or how to go about figuring that out.

Papers— Applications, Resumes, and More 3

There are two keys to a successful job hunt—one is deal-ing with paper, the other involves people. This chapter is about paper. In many cases, employers see the papers you have prepared about yourself long before they meet you. You will fill out an application or send in a resume. Based on that application or resume you will be called to the next step, the interview, or you will be eliminated. Often the same is true after you leave the interview. Your appli-cation or resume is left behind as the only concrete re-minder of your skills and personality. This chapter will help you present yourself in the best possible light so that your strengths stand out on paper and the very ap-pearance of the papers themselves show how well orga-nized you are.

The first section of this chapter provides directions on how to complete job applications and the information you should have on hand whenever you expect to complete one. The second section gives you suggestions for preparing your resume and cover letter and examples that you can use as models. Some jobs, particularly civil service jobs, require tests. The third section of this chapter gives you some hints on taking tests. In the fourth section of the chapter, helpful hints on items to take with you on your job hunt are given.

How to Complete Job Applications

Although many companies have job applications that are made particularly for them, most applications ask for the same information. In general, this includes the following:

- Location information—your name, address, and telephone number; and the name, address, and telephone number of someone to contact in an emergency

- Your Social Security number

- Job desired—the name of the position for which you are applying, are you looking for full-time or part-time work, the date you are available for work, the salary you expect, the source of your application or how you heard of the company, relatives who work for the company

- Education information—the degrees you have, where you went to school, when you graduated, what you majored in

- Work history—jobs you have held, when you held them, where you worked

- Special skills and talents—typing ability, knowledge of foreign languages, hobbies, volunteer work, sports, honors and awards in school

- References—the names and addresses of three people who can discuss your strengths and abilities

- Citizenship and military service

- Criminal records

As soon as you decide to apply for a job you need to be prepared to complete an application. You may be going to a company office because one of the employment services suggested in chapter 2 has sent you to apply for a job; you may be going because you identified the company as one that has the kind of work you want to do; or you may be going because you are answering a newspaper ad. Here are six tips for completing a job application.

Six tips for completing a job application

1. Have all your information prepared ahead of time and carry it with you so that you know the answers to all the questions that apply to you. **Be accurate.**

2. Always apply for a specific job title. In the space "Position Desired," never write "anything." There is no job called "anything," so no one will know what to do with your application. **Be definite.**

3. Answer all questions honestly. **Be honest.**

4. Don't leave any blanks. If a question does not apply to you, write "No" or "None" or "Not Applicable." **Be complete.**

5. Sometimes you are asked to complete your work history or education history in chronological order; this means you start with the first and move to the most recent. Sometimes you are asked for reverse chronological order; this means you start with the most recent and present things going backward in time. **Read directions.**

6. Complete the application in ink. Carry a pen with an ink eraser or even some correction fluid. **Neatness counts.**

In the following pages, you will find three worksheets to help you complete job applications. First, there is a sample job application that has been completed correctly for you to use as a model. Of course, your answers to the questions will be different. Then there is a blank job application for you to complete. Finally there is a worksheet for you to complete and carry with you when you go job hunting. Completing this worksheet ahead of time and taking it with you will give you the information you need when you need it.

Sample Job Application Form

Date of Application ~~9-1-84 92~~ 7-1-92   Social Security No. 123-45-6789

Full Name (Last, First) YEE, SANDRA

Address 6105 DAWN ROAD

City INDIANAPOLIS   State INDIANA   Zip 46240

Home Telephone (317) 442-1010   Business Telephone NONE

Position Applied For FULL CHARGE BOOKKEEPER

Referred By INDIANAPOLIS COMMUNITY COLLEGE PLACEMENT

When will you be available to begin work? IMMEDIATELY

Can you travel if the job requires it? YES

Have you been employed here before? No   If Yes, Give Date —

Have you applied for a job here before? No   If Yes, Give Date —

Are you a United States citizen? YES

If no, do you have an alien registration card and will you produce it for inspection? —

If you are a veteran of the U. S. Military Service, give dates of service and branch. NA

Have you been convicted of a crime in the last seven years? No

If Yes, Give Date NA   Place NA   Offense NA

Education:	Name and Address of School	No. of Years Attended	Did you Graduate	Major/Degree
High School	RIPPLE HS 855 E. 59 ST INDIANAPOLIS	4	YES	ACADEMIC
College	INDIANAPOLIS COMMUNITY COLLEGE 7331 STATION ST	2	YES	ACCOUNTING
Trade School or Other	NONE			
Special Training	NONE			

Employment History (Start with your most recent position)

Name & Address of Employer or Organization	Dates Employed From Month/Year To Month/Year	Nature of Work	Reason for Leaving	Name of Supervisor	Salary
CORN + MORE SUPERMARKET 420 W. NEW YORK ST. INDIANAPOLIS	9/85- 88- 5/87 90	BOOKKEEPER	PART-TIME WHILE IN COLLEGE	NEAL McKINLAY	$5.00/ per hour
COALITION FOR THE HOMELESS 4015 E 32 ST INDIANAPOLIS	SUMMER 84 86 91-92	ASSISTED IN INVENTORIES OF FOOD	SUMMER VOLUNTEER WORK	JANICE BLOCK	NA

NA

NA

References (Other than supervisors listed above)

Name	Full Address	Telephone	Relationship
CHARLES ECKBERG	ACCOUNTING DEPARTMENT INDIANAPOLIS CC 7331 STATION ST	274-5990	PROFESSOR
MARTHA FULLER	PHYSICAL EDUC. DEPT. INDIANAPOLIS CC 7331 STATION ST	274-5991	PROFESSOR
BRIAN COUNTS	ENGLISH DEPARTMENT INDIANAPOLIS CC 7331 STATION ST	274-5994	PROFESSOR

Special Skills (foreign languages, licenses, association memberships)

CAPTAIN OF COLLEGE FENCING TEAM

If you have ever been known by any other name, please indicate.

NONE

Sample Job Application Form

Date of Application _____ Social Security No._____

Full Name (Last, First) _____

Address _____

City _____ State _____ Zip _____

Home Telephone _____ Business Telephone _____

Position Applied For _____

Referred By _____

When will you be available to begin work? _____

Can you travel if the job requires it? _____

Have you been employed here before? _____ If Yes, Give Date _____

Have you applied for a job here before? _____ If Yes, Give Date _____

Are you a United States citizen? _____

If no, do you have an alien registration card and will you produce it for inspection? _____

If you are a veteran of the U. S. Military Service, give dates of service and branch. _____

Have you been convicted of a crime in the last seven years? _____

If Yes, Give Date _____ Place _____ Offense _____

Education:	Name and Address of School	No. of Years Attended	Did You Graduate	Major/Degree
High School				
College				
Trade School or Other				
Special Training				

Employment History (Start with your most recent position)

Name & Address of Employer or Organization	Dates Employed From Month/Year To Month/Year	Nature of Work	Reason for Leaving	Name of Supervisor	Salary

----

References (Other than supervisors listed above)

Name	Full Address	Telephone	Relationship

Special Skills (foreign languages, licenses, association memberships)

If you have ever been known by any other name, please indicate.

Job Information Worksheet

Complete the information in this worksheet and tear it out or copy it so that you can carry it with you for reference when you complete job applications.

Name (Use only your legal names, not nicknames)

_____

Other Names You Have Used Legally _____

Address: Building Number & Street _____

_____

City, State, and Zip Code _____

_____

Telephone Number at Home _____

Social Security Number _____

Job Title _____

Date You Are Available _____

Education: High School _____

Dates Attended: From _____ to _____

Type of Diploma _____

Major (if any) _____

Education: College _____

Dates Attended: From _____ to _____

Type of Diploma _____

Major _____

Education: Technical School _____

Dates Attended: From _____ to _____

Type of Diploma _____

Major _____

Education: Other _____

Dates Attended: From _____ to _____

Type of Diploma _____

Major (if any) _____

Work History (Use this space to include part-time and volunteer work)

Job 1: Name of Company or Organization _____

Address _____

Type of Work _____

Reason for Leaving _____

Dates of Employment _____

Name of Supervisor _____

Job 2: Name of Company or Organization _____

Address _____

Type of Work _____

Reason for Leaving _____

Dates of Employment _____

Name of Supervisor _____

Job 3: Name of Company or Organization _____

Address _____

Type of Work _____

Reason for Leaving _____

Dates of Employment _____

Name of Supervisor _____

Special Skills (List typing wpm, foreign languages, knowledge of computers, sports, awards, and any others) _____

_____

_____

Dates of Military Service (if any) _____

References: (Include people who know the strengths an employer might be interested in—teachers, members of the clergy, people you have worked with or for. You can give their business addresses, such as the school they work in. Be sure to ask each person for permission. Do not list relatives such as aunts or cousins.)

Name 1 _____

Business or Organization (if applicable) _____

Street Address _____

City, State, Zip _____

Telephone Number _____

Relationship to You (teacher, friend, colleague, supervisor, etc.) _____

Name 2 _____

Business or Organization (if applicable) _____

Street Address _____

City, State, Zip _____

Telephone Number _____

Relationship to You _____

Name 3 _____

Business or Organization (if applicable) _____

Street Address _____

City, State, Zip _____

Telephone Number _____

Relationship to You _____

Criminal Record (if any) (This includes only convictions—not arrests, youthful offender, or minor traffic violations.)

Date _____

Place _____

Offense _____

Disposition _____

Writing Resumes and Cover Letters

When you answer an ad in a newspaper, you are often asked to send a resume. A resume is a brief statement of your accomplishments. Your goal is to have a winning resume, one that gets you to the next step, the job interview. Every resume must have a cover letter to go with it. The first part of this section explains resumes; the second is about cover letters.

Employers in a variety of industries were asked what recommendations as to resume writing they would give to a young person applying for her or his first job. They offered two major pieces of advice. The first was to be as concise as possible. The second was to be factual and down-to-earth. Some specific suggestions were as follows:

- "List only real achievements. If you have none, write a sincere cover letter stating your goals and your willingness to work hard."

- "Make the resume fit the job. There is no resume that will fit every job."

- "I like to see how well one got through school—interests, honors, energy."

- "If I get a resume of more than two pages from a young person, I'm getting fluff. Either the person can't write or it's baloney."

- "Be honest. Be factual. Avoid exaggeration at all costs."

Since you are looking for your first full-time job, your resume will be brief. You will use it to try to show that you have energy and initiative in whatever you do. Creation of a winning resume, one that gets you an interview, has five steps.

Five steps to a winning resume

1. Examine the relevant areas of your life in depth, making notes as you go. By writing out the details, you get the material that you need to write a comprehensive, convincing resume. Worksheet spaces are provided in the following pages for you to develop this raw material.

2. Translate the details into the best language for a resume. This language consists of action words, verbs, and vocabulary related to the field of work in which you are job hunting. You can look at the sample resume in this chapter for some examples of this. You can also go to job descriptions in computer-based career information systems or in books to get a feel for the language. If you are in school or working with a counselor, he or she can help you with this.

3. Select the parts of the resume you want and write a rough draft of it.

4. Arrange your resume on the page so that it is easy to read and attractive. You may need to type it several times until it looks the best it can.

5. Proofread your resume. Eliminate all spelling and typographical errors. If you are not good at seeing spelling or usage errors, get help from someone who is. A resume with errors or one that has sloppy corrections or black marks from photocopying will *not* get you an interview. Employers will think that you just don't care about working for them, or if you do care, that you can't tell a good job from a poor one.

The possible sections of a resume are explained in the following resume worksheets. Use the blank spaces after each section to fill in information about yourself. After the worksheets, you will find a good sample resume. Using the worksheet sections and their explanations, decide what should be in your resume. Use the sample resume as a model for layout.

This chapter gives you some information about resume writing. It would be silly to pretend that this is all that can be said about resumes when there are many books on this subject alone. Be sure to consult other books on resume writing if you feel you need more guidance and information. *How to Write a Winning Résumé* (VGM Career Horizons) is a good book to use.

You will note, as you look over the worksheets, that there is no place for your age, marital status, or physical characteristics. That is because it is against the law to include these as factors in job selection. Race, religion, and national origin are other factors that may not be considered. You will want to remember this in your interviews and throughout the job-hunting process. You may also notice that there is no place for a job objective. That belongs in the cover letter, which will be explained in the next part of this chapter. There is also no place for a summary or highlights. The entire resume *is* a summary.

Resume Worksheet 1—The Heading

The heading is an essential section. It must include your name, home address, and telephone number. If you can receive calls at work, include your business number. This makes it easier for people to reach you during the business day.

Name _____

Full Address _____

_____

_____

Telephone Numbers _____

_____

_____

Resume Worksheet 2—Education

Education is also an essential section. Include the degrees you have earned, the institutions at which you earned them, and the dates of attendance. List your most advanced degree first. You should also list any courses taken to upgrade or enhance your skills. Finally, if you were awarded any honors in school, list them. Also include any special course work you took or projects you did. Use these to show unusual accomplishment or energy. Do not list the regular courses of study for your field. The person reading the resume will just see that as an attempt to puff yourself up.

College _____

    Dates Attended: From_____ to _____

    Type of Diploma _____

    Major _____

    Special Projects _____

    _____

    Evidence of Leadership _____

    _____

    Awards or Honors _____

Technical School _____

    Dates Attended: From_____ to _____

    Type of Diploma _____

    Major _____

Special Projects _____

_____

Evidence of Leadership _____

_____

Awards or Honors _____

High School _____

    Dates Attended: From_____ to _____

    Type of Diploma _____

    Major (if any) _____

    Special Projects _____

_____

    Evidence of Leadership _____

_____

    Awards or Honors _____

Other _____

    Dates Attended: From_____ to _____

    Type of Diploma _____

    Major (if any) _____

    Special Projects _____

_____

    Evidence of Leadership _____

_____

    Awards or Honors _____

Other _____

    Dates Attended: From_____ to _____

    Type of Diploma _____

    Major (if any) _____

    Special Projects _____

_____

    Evidence of Leadership _____

_____

    Awards or Honors _____

Resume Worksheet 3—Work History

Work history should be included if you have held any part-time or summer jobs. They show that you know how to work. It should include each of your jobs, beginning with the most recent. For each job, include the dates you were there, the company, and your title. List your major duties and responsibilities.

Job 1: Name of Company or Organization _____

    Address _____

    Type of Work _____

    Dates of Employment _____

    Major Duties and Responsibilities _____

    _____

    Most Important Accomplishment _____

Job 2: Name of Company or Organization _____

    Address _____

    Type of Work _____

    Dates of Employment _____

    Major Duties and Responsibilities _____

    _____

    Most Important Accomplishment _____

Job 3: Name of Company or Organization _____

    Address _____

    Type of Work _____

    Dates of Employment _____

    Major Duties and Responsibilities _____

    _____

    Most Important Accomplishment _____

Job 4: Name of Company or Organization _____

    Address _____

    Type of Work _____

    Dates of Employment _____

    Major Duties and Responsibilities _____

    _____

    Most Important Accomplishment _____

Resume Worksheet 4—Licenses and Certificates

Professional licenses and certificates is an essential section if these are required for the kind of work you do. Give the title, issuing agency, and date of issuance for each license you hold.

Title of License _____

Issued by _____

Date of Issue _____

Title of License _____

Issued by _____

Date of Issue _____

Title of License _____

Issued by _____

Date of Issue _____

Title of License _____

Issued by _____

Date of Issue _____

Title of License _____

Issued by _____

Date of Issue _____

Resume Worksheet 5—Volunteer Activities

    Volunteer activities should be included only if you have activities that show enthusiasm, energy, and a high level of interest. These are characteristics employers like. If your hobbies are only of passing interest to you, do not include this section. When the potential employer starts to talk to you about them in the interview, your lack of real interest will be a strike against you. Use this section to show work that you have done for which you have not been paid or to show hobbies or sports that are really important to you.

_____

_____

_____

_____

_____

_____

_____

_____

_____

_____

_____

_____

_____

_____

_____

_____

_____

_____

Resume Worksheet 6—Special Abilities

Special abilities is an optional section that you should include if you have abilities related to your work, such as a knowledge of foreign languages or computer programming. In general, these are listed after the work history. If you are looking for a job in the computer field, your knowledge of programming languages and computer systems should be the first item after the heading.

_____

_____

_____

_____

_____

_____

_____

_____

_____

_____

_____

_____

_____

_____

_____

_____

_____

Sample Resume

Resume

Philip Juarez
571 Vermont Street
Brooklyn, New York 11207
(718) 555-3450

EDUCATION

Albert Einstein High School, Diploma, June 1990
Major: Merchandising
Specialized Courses: Retailing, Fashion Communications, Data Processing, Junior
                             Achievement Economics, Art Electives in Display and Package Design

WORK EXPERIENCE

1989–present   STOCK CLERK   Blooms Department Store
                                                                                    New York, New York

Stock shelves, monitor supplies on the floor to see what is needed, take inventory, assist in
unpacking and packing. (Part-time work while in school.)

Summer 1988   MAINTENANCE WORKER   Parks Department
                                                                                    New York, New York

Participated in all indoor and outdoor cleanup activities in various parts of Central Park.

OTHER ACTIVITIES

Worked in the school boutique for two years. The school boutique workers are responsible for
purchasing merchandise for sale to students, pricing the items, and then working behind the
counter selling to students. In the boutique, I moved from being a general worker to being a
member of the committee responsible for merchandise selection.

In the Junior Achievement economics class, I worked on a project to select a product and market it.
Our group made the largest profit in the class.

SKILLS

Familiar with the IBM PC. Can use data processing and word processing software.

Type 35 WPM.

Now that you have finished your resume, you must prepare a cover letter, which tells employers why you are sending them your resume. Remember that the cover letter is designed to introduce the resume and interest your potential employer in reading your resume, just as the resume is designed to interest that person in meeting you. The cover letter must be neat and clean in both content and production.

Seven sections of the cover letter

1. Your address (unless it is typed on your personal letterhead, which already includes this information).

2. The date.

3. The inside address of the person and company to whom you are sending the resume. If you are addressing a box number in an advertisement, include the box number information and the line *To whom it may concern:*.

4. The first paragraph should explain why you are writing this letter. Is it in response to an advertisement, the result of a previous meeting, or at the suggestion of someone who is helping you through your networking contacts?

5. The second paragraph should present one or two highlights of your experience in terms of what you believe to be the requirements of the job or needs of the company.

6. The final paragraph should close with a request for an interview and any pertinent information needed to schedule the interview. This might include hours during which you can be reached at a particular telephone number.

7. Whether the letter is to be sent to a classified ad box or to an individual, the correct closing is, *Sincerely,* or *Yours truly,* followed by your signature, followed by your full name typed out.

The cover letter must always be an individually typed, one-page document on good, 8 1/2″ × 11″ bond paper. Since the cover letters must be written to particular individuals or at least to particular companies, they cannot be reproduced or photocopied like resumes. Of course, once you have written and rewritten your first cover letter to the point where you really like it and feel it represents you well, you may certainly use the same or similar wording in subsequent letters to other prospective employers.

After you have typed your cover letter, proofread it as thoroughly as you did the resume. Handle it carefully to avoid a dirty appearance. Mail the cover letter and resume in an envelope of the appropriate size. A sample of a good cover letter follows:

Sample Cover Letter

571 Vermont Street
Brooklyn, New York 11207
August 11, 1992

Ajax Merchandising Consortium
1407 Seventh Avenue
New York, New York 10011

Personnel Manager:

I am enclosing my resume in response to your advertisement in the New York Times of August 10th for an assistant to the buyer of children's wear.

As you can see from my resume, I have had experience in school in purchasing, and courses in merchandising, fashion, and office procedures that I believe will be helpful in this job.

I am currently working part-time in a department store, but I am enthusiastic about beginning full-time work in the field I have prepared for. I would appreciate the opportunity to meet with you at your convenience. I can be reached at home in the mornings and most evenings at (718) 555-3450.

Sincerely,

Philip Juarez

Philip Juarez

Taking Tests to Get a Job

You may have hoped that once you were out of school you would never have to take a test again. However, many jobs require tests as part of their application procedures. Almost all civil service jobs require tests. In addition, many secretarial or office jobs require tests of typing or clerical abilities. It is impossible to predict whether or not a particular employer is going to ask you to take a test, but you can be prepared. This section will give you some ways to do that.

First, be aware that tests can take several forms. You can be asked to answer questions in writing or by filling in answer blanks. You may be asked to perform some task, such as typing a document. You may be asked in an interview situation to talk about what you would do in particular circumstances. Whatever the type of test, it will be related to the job you will be performing. Therefore, if you are prepared for the job, you will pass the test.

Most civil service jobs require tests. You can study for these ahead of time by getting books that describe the tests and give sample questions and answers. One book, for example, is *The Civil Service Handbook* (ARCO). ARCO is a company that publishes many of these kinds of books. There is probably at least one book for every type of test given. Of course, it is difficult to prepare well at the last minute. So if you are considering a civil service job, get the appropriate book and begin work as soon as you can.

If you are applying for jobs that require skills such as typing or driving, expect to be tested. Practice before you go to the employer so you are prepared to be tested.

Whenever you go for a test for a job, whether the job is in civil service or business, follow these simple hints.

Five hints for test taking

1. Learn all you can about the test before you go to take it.

2. Study from test preparation books or practice your skills.

3. Know what tools you need for the test, and bring them with you. This *always* includes at least four sharpened pencils and two pens with blue or black ink.

4. Know the time you are supposed to be at the test and the location. Be sure you know how to travel to the location. Get there about twenty minutes earlier than you are scheduled to.

5. Get a good night's sleep before the test, and eat a solid breakfast on the day of the test.

When an organization is considering offering you a job, they may ask you to take a physical exam or a drug-use test or a polygraph (lie detector) test. It is your right to refuse to take the test. However, you can be pretty sure that you will not get the job if you do not take the test.

Additional Papers for Your Job Search

In addition to the papers already identified—the application, the resume, the cover letter, and tests—you will need some personal papers during your job search. Some employers will ask for these during the application process. Others may want them as soon as you are hired. It is a good idea to have these ready as soon as you begin job hunting.

Your *Social Security card* is your ticket to work in the United States. You cannot be employed without one. To get a Social Security card, go to any district office of the Social Security Administration. Bring a copy of your birth or baptismal certificate to attach to the application. It will take six to eight weeks to get a card, so apply for one right away. Once you have a card, put one copy away in a safe place and keep the other with your job application worksheet information. You will often need your Social Security number, so write it in several places that you can get to easily.

A *Selective Service Registration Acknowledgment* form may be required of you if you are male. The law requires that all men register within one month of their 18th birthday. You can register at your local United States Post Office. If you have finished military service, you should have your discharge papers.

High school or college diplomas and *copies of your current transcripts or grade reports* may be asked for to prove the statements on your application and to show your grades. Have copies of these ready, and take them with you.

Your *birth certificate* or *baptismal certificate* may be required to prove your age and citizenship.

Citizenship papers, an *alien registration receipt card,* often called a *Green Card,* or other appropriate proof of your right to work in the United States should be available if you were not born a United States citizen.

A *work permit* should be carried if you are under 18 years of age. You can find out the particular requirements in your state from a local state employment service office.

A *union card,* if you have one, should be carried.

A *portfolio* of your work, if you are in an art-related field, is also appropriate.

The *job application worksheets* with your information should be on hand whenever you go to apply for a job so that you are not caught not knowing enough about yourself.

A resume, if you have prepared one, should be carried so that you can leave it as a reminder to people you have met.

As you look over the list of papers, you will see that you want to carry some with you as you go to employers and that you will want to have others ready at home. If you have a briefcase, carry the papers in a folder or envelope inside the case. If you prefer not to carry a briefcase, get a sturdy manila envelope that will hold all of your papers. Remember to carry sharpened pencils and a pen with blue or black ink with you all the time. Now that you have finished working on your papers, you are ready to move to the next step, job interviews.

Summary Worksheet

In this chapter, you learned how to prepare the papers for a job search. Use the checklist that follows to be sure you have covered all bases.

_____I have a Social Security card.

_____I know what to expect to see on a job application.

_____I have prepared my personal information to complete a job application.

_____I know the six tips for completing a job application.

_____I have prepared my resume.

_____I have proofread my resume and there are no mistakes.

_____I have proofread my resume *again* and I am sure there are no mistakes.

_____I know what to include in a cover letter with my resume.

_____I am ready to take the appropriate tests for the job I want.

_____I have gone over the list of suggested items to carry on a job search.

_____I know which ones to carry all the time and which ones to have ready at home.

_____I am ready to think about job interviews.

People—Seven Steps to a Winning Interview

Once you have identified some places to look for a job and you have begun filling out applications and sending resumes, you can expect to be called for interviews. This chapter will take you through the seven steps to a winning interview, an interview that gets you the job you want. This does not mean you will get the first job for which you are interviewed. Most people go through many interviews before they get the right job. Many of them report, however, that they get better and better at it with practice.

The research for this chapter included discussions with employers in a variety of industries including advertising, accounting, banking, merchandising, and computers. They stressed the importance of preparing for an interview so that you can present your skills and experiences in a way that has meaning for the employer. These seven steps will help you do that.

It is important to remember that an interview is not a contest between you and the employer. A winning interview means that you both end up on the same team. Listed below are the seven steps that will put you on the winning team. The rest of the chapter gives you more information on how to carry out each of the steps and provides you with worksheets that will help you prepare for your interview.

Seven steps to a winning interview

1. Get all the preliminary information you need when you make the appointment for an interview.

2. Assess your own strengths and weaknesses.

3. Learn all that you can about the job and the company or organization.

4. Think about how your skills fit the job.

5. Plan how you will look as carefully as you plan what to say.

6. Accept your nervousness, and turn nervous energy into positive energy.

7. Know the kinds of questions you will probably be asked and how to answer them.

Making the Interview Appointment

You are now at the stage where you are ready to make arrangements. This means you have developed enough interest in a potential employer so that he or she is willing to spend some time with you. You may have done this through networking contacts, through referral by an employment service of one type or another, or by writing in answer to an advertisement or some other type of lead.

Generally speaking, you will receive a telephone call from a member of the personnel department or from a secretary representing the person who will interview you. Sometimes you will get a letter asking you to telephone, and sometimes you will get a letter asking you to come at a specific time. Sometimes you are the one who makes the first telephone call if you are answering a newspaper advertisement that says to call rather than to write.

As soon as you send out your first resume or make your first contact, you should be ready to accept the invitation to an interview. To do this, you need to think about the information you will need so that you will be in the right place at the right time, prepared to do your best. Listed below are the eight items of information you need.

Eight items of information you need before the interview

1. The name of the company

2. The street address of the company

3. Travel directions

4. The name of the person you are going to see

5. The room number of that person

6. The date and time of the interview

7. The name of the person to whom you are speaking

8. The telephone number of that person

In many cases, the person who will interview you is not part of a personnel department, and the secretary calling you is not particularly familiar with making arrangements for an employment interview. You must take the responsibility for getting the information you need.

It is often so exciting when the call for an interview comes that it is difficult to remember all your needs during the call. But you must! Keep the following Interview Arrangements Worksheets handy, and use them when you get the call. Make more copies if you need them. If you might get some calls at work and some at home, keep copies in both places. Be sure you have all the spellings and pronunciations correct before you hang up. Remember, it is better to ask to have something repeated than to go into the interview addressing Mr. Baily as "Mr. Quail."

Notice that the Interview Arrangements Worksheets end with a place for results and follow-up. Save these worksheets to keep track of the developments in your job hunt.

Interview Arrangements Worksheet 1

Name of Organization _____

Street Address _____

Room Number _____

Date _____

Travel Directions _____

_____

_____

Name of Interviewer _____

Title of Interviewer _____

Person Making Arrangements _____

Telephone Number _____

Materials to Bring _____

_____

Additional Notes _____

_____

_____

_____

Other People I Met _____

_____

_____

_____

Results of Interview _____

_____

_____

Next Steps _____

_____

_____

Interview Arrangements Worksheet 2

Name of Organization _____

Street Address _____

Room Number _____

Date _____

Travel Directions _____

_____

_____

Name of Interviewer _____

Title of Interviewer _____

Person Making Arrangements _____

Telephone Number _____

Materials to Bring _____

_____

Additional Notes _____

_____

_____

_____

Other People I Met _____

_____

_____

_____

Results of Interview _____

_____

_____

Next Steps _____

_____

_____

Interview Arrangements Worksheet 3

Name of Organization _____

Street Address _____

Room Number _____

Date _____

Travel Directions _____

_____

_____

Name of Interviewer _____

Title of Interviewer _____

Person Making Arrangements _____

Telephone Number _____

Materials to Bring _____

_____

Additional Notes _____

_____

_____

_____

Other People I Met _____

_____

_____

_____

Results of Interview _____

_____

_____

Next Steps _____

_____

_____

Interview Arrangements Worksheet 4

Name of Organization _____

Street Address _____

Room Number _____

Date _____

Travel Directions _____

_____

_____

Name of Interviewer _____

Title of Interviewer _____

Person Making Arrangements _____

Telephone Number _____

Materials to Bring _____

_____

Additional Notes _____

_____

_____

_____

Other People I Met _____

_____

_____

_____

Results of Interview _____

_____

_____

Next Steps _____

_____

_____

Assessing Your Strengths and Weaknesses

Before you can go into an interview and let someone else know what your strengths are and how you can overcome any weaknesses that you have, you have to understand these things yourself. Just as you had to think about a lot of information to prepare your resume, you need to do this before the job interview. Once you have done this, you will be ready to think about the skills that are needed on the job you are seeking and how to match your skills to those needed.

There are three worksheets on the pages that follow. The first one asks you to think of skills you have developed in various activities in your life. Remember, you may be looking for your first full-time, paid job, but you have been working for a long time. You have worked in school. You may have worked at a part-time job. Perhaps you worked in community or volunteer activities. Think also of jobs you have done for your own family, even though you may not have been paid for them. The second worksheet gives a list of traits that employers said they found important. You are asked to think of whether you have these traits and what examples you have from any area of your life. The last worksheet in this section asks you to assess honestly any weaknesses you have and how you can overcome them. In all of this, try to think of strengths and weaknesses as they relate to the kind of job you wish to find.

Strength Assessment Worksheet 1

I have acquired the following job skills in school:

Skill   **Program, Course, or Other Source**
EXAMPLE: Know word processing   Took word processing 1 and 2

_____   _____

_____   _____

_____   _____

_____   _____

_____   _____

I have acquired the following job skills in part-time work:

Skill   **Job Responsibility**
EXAMPLE: Patience   Cleaning up in the park

_____   _____

_____   _____

_____   _____

_____   _____

_____   _____

I have acquired the following job skills in volunteer, leisure, or family activities:

Skill   **Activity**
EXAMPLE: Persuasion   I collected funds for the Red Cross

_____   _____

_____   _____

_____   _____

_____   _____

_____   _____

Strength Assessment Worksheet 2

Listed below are ten traits. Put a check next to each one that is true of you, and describe how you used each trait in some work, school, or other activity.

Trait   **Activity**

_____ Teamworker   _____
                                                        _____
                                                        _____

_____ Tactful   _____
                                                        _____
                                                        _____

_____ Able to change   _____
                                                        _____
                                                        _____

_____ Able to start things on my own   _____
                                                        _____
                                                        _____

_____ Self-disciplined   _____
                                                        _____
                                                        _____

_____ Follow through on work   _____
                                                        _____
                                                        _____

_____ Hard worker   _____
                                                        _____
                                                        _____

_____ Honest and sincere   _____
                                                        _____
                                                        _____

_____ Able to think clearly under pressure   _____
                                                        _____
                                                        _____

_____ Get along well with others   _____
                                                        _____
                                                        _____

Strength Assessment Worksheet 3

What do you consider your three greatest weaknesses and how are you working to overcome them? (Knowing your weaknesses, not pretending you are Superman or Wonder Woman, helps you identify your strengths.)

Weakness   **I am overcoming it by:**

EXAMPLE: Losing my temper   Learning to count slowly to ten

1. _____   _____

   _____   _____

   _____   _____

                                                      _____

                                                      _____

2. _____   _____

   _____   _____

   _____   _____

                                                      _____

                                                      _____

3. _____   _____

   _____   _____

   _____   _____

                                                      _____

                                                      _____

Learning About the Job

Before you go for a job interview, you need to be able to look at things from an employer's point of view. Looking at things from the employer's point of view will help you answer questions so that your answers are meaningful to her or to him. When you are in school, you are often called on to answer questions with right answers, answers that center on you. In the job interview, the right answer always centers on the job and how you relate to it.

If you are using any of the employment services discussed in chapter 2, you can receive help from the counselors in getting information about the jobs you are applying for and about the company or organizations that are offering these jobs. You can also use the general sources in the library that have been mentioned—computer-based career information delivery systems and printed information that describes jobs in general. If you know anyone who is in a similar job or who works for the company to which you will be applying, talk to that person for information.

The following job information worksheet gives you an idea of the kinds of questions you will want to know about each job. You may want to duplicate the worksheet before you fill it in, since you will probably apply for more than one job before you are offered a job that you accept.

Job Information Worksheet

1. What is the major product or service of this organization?

_____

_____

2. How does the job I am seeking contribute to this product or service?

_____

_____

_____

3. What are the major responsibilities of the job I am seeking?

_____

_____

_____

4. What skills or knowledge does someone need to carry out these responsibilities?

_____

_____

_____

_____

_____

5. Which of these skills or knowledge do I have?

_____

_____

_____

_____

_____

Matching Your Skills to the Job

If you filled in the Job Information Worksheet, you have already begun to think about how your skills and knowledge fit the job you are seeking. In the worksheet that follows, you will bring together what you have learned about yourself and about the job.

Bringing these together and concentrating on them when giving your answers will produce a winning interview. Sometimes employers ask general questions, like "Tell me about yourself." They really want to know about you in relation to their job. This is an opportunity to take information from the Job Match Worksheet that follows and talk about it. You will be able to say something like, "I understand that one of the major responsibilities of this job is delivering materials to many building sites around town. I really know this town well and can get around easily. I took driver's education courses, and I am a careful driver. I have never had any traffic violations."

Job Match Worksheet

Job Requirement	My Qualifications	Proof
Example: Able to handle and keep track of cash	Trustworthy Used to dealing with money	Treasurer of Junior Baseball League

Planning for a Good First Impression

Like it or not, the first impression anyone has of you is a visual one. You want to use that to your advantage so that your appearance makes the interviewer, your potential employer, want to listen to you.

All of the employers questioned about interviews said pretty much the same thing. They want to see someone who is neat and clean and whose appearance shows that they know what the working world expects. There are some definite things you can do to create the appearance of caring about the job and knowing your way in business.

An employer simply will not want to hire someone to take care of a job who has not learned to take care of herself or himself. Here are some good grooming tips.

Hair care tips

Your hair should be neatly and attractively cut. If you have a problem with dandruff, ask your pharmacist to help you select a special shampoo.

Teeth tips

Clean teeth are the result of ongoing good dental care. If you don't have clean teeth, you probably have bad breath. If you have bad breath, interviewers will spend their time turning away from you rather than listening to you. See your dentist to be sure your teeth are in good condition. Floss and brush your teeth twice a day. Be sure to brush your teeth right before going for an interview.

Bad breath can also be caused by eating a lot of garlic or onions. Some people hold on to these odors for a long time. Your best bet is not to eat dishes with garlic or onions the day before an interview.

If you are not sure of your breath, suck on a mint just before the interview, but be sure to finish it or throw it away before you get into the office. All of the employers said that chewing gum or eating candy during the interview was one of the fastest ways *not* to get hired.

Hand tips

Be sure that your hands are clean and your nails are well manicured. This does not mean you have to use polish. Just be sure your nails are clipped evenly, the cuticles are trimmed, and there is no dirt under the nails.

Since it is your goal to attract the interviewer to your ideas, not your hands, it is a good idea, if you are a woman, to wear only clear or very light polish.

Body tips   Be sure to shower or bathe the day of an interview. Use deodorant. If you have particularly heavy perspiration, use an antiperspirant.

Clothing tips   Select clothing that shows you know you are in a business situation. Ask yourself this question: Do people who hold jobs like the one I want usually wear suits to work?

If the answer is "yes" and you are a man, wear a suit with a shirt and tie to the interview. Your shoes should be similarly formal in style. Do not wear sneakers or casual moccasins with a suit.

If the answer is "yes" and you are a woman, then you should wear a tailored suit, blouse, and dress shoes.

If the answer is "no, people would not usually wear suits to this job," you have a little more freedom in what you wear. However, remember, it is always better to be more conservative when you go for a job interview. A man can wear neatly pressed slacks with a sport jacket or sweater. If you are a woman, you can wear a skirt and blouse or a tailored dress.

The clothes you wear should also make you feel good about yourself. Sometimes it is the color of clothes that gives us a special feeling. Sometimes it is the way they fit. Try to choose clothes that make you feel good or cheerful.

Be sure your clothes have been freshly laundered or dry cleaned for each interview. There will be no chance then of spots or of lingering body odor.

Accessory tips   The key word in accessories is moderation. Remember, you want to draw attention to your thoughts, not your earrings. If you want to wear jewelry, keep it small and simple. If you wear scent—perfume or after-shave lotion—keep it light.

Accepting and Using Nervousness   A number of people who were recently hired were asked about their experiences in the job interview process. Every single one of them said that he or she was nervous. However, each of them had also found a way to use the nervous energy or to control it.

Here are some of the answers that the successful job applicants gave.

- "I know I need rest. I need to relax physically. The day before an interview, I didn't run around shopping. I went home, read the paper, and got a good night's sleep."

- "I just focus on getting there. Then I walk to the interview. That gets rid of a lot of tension."

- "I go through a lot of normal stuff like before a test. I try to plan the interview in my mind, think of the questions I might be asked. Also dressing well makes me feel confident."

- "I rely on thinking of the actor's saying. It's something like, 'If you're nervous before you go onstage, you won't be nervous onstage and if you're not nervous before you go onstage, you're in trouble.' I really just let the nervousness happen. All the nervousness beforehand gets you prepared, psyched."

- "I use a little meditation and visualization. I picture myself being calm and having an easy flowing conversation with another human being."

You may have some ways you already use to help yourself in tension-producing situations. If you want to learn more techniques for doing this, read the book *Creative Visualization* by Shakti Gawain (Bantam Books). If you want more information about how to use these techniques specifically for interviews as well as more information on all of the interview preparation steps, read *How to Have a Winning Job Interview* (VGM Career Horizons).

Answering the Questions

If you think ahead of time about the kinds of questions you will be asked, it is easier to be prepared with the answers you want to give. There are three basic kinds of questions employers will ask.

Three types of interview questions

1. *The specific question*—some examples are:

   - What were your major courses of study?
   - Why did you choose those courses?
   - What was the most important thing you learned in school?
   - Do you plan to continue your education?
   - Do you feel your education was worthwhile?
   - What did you learn in _____ (some experience on your resume or application)?
   - (After a description of the job) How do you see yourself fitting in with this job?

2. *The general question*—some examples are:

   - Tell me about yourself.
   - Why do you think you are the best person for this job?
   - Why do you want this job?
   - Is there anything else about you that you would like me to know?

3. *The problem question*—in this type of question, the employer describes a situation that you might come across on the job and asks you how you would handle it.

To answer a specific question, be specific. Suppose you were asked, "What was your most important course in school?" Do not answer, "Lunch." Do not answer "Gym," unless you are applying for a job in recreation. Answer with the name of a course or several courses related to the job you are seeking. Explain why this course was important to you then and now. Here is a good answer:

> The most important course I took was "Introduction to Word Processing." It really helped me see how computers can be used not only to type letters but to make office work more efficient in so many ways.

General questions are harder to answer. Interviewers often use general questions to see what you will choose to say.

When asked a general question, you have to make a series of quick choices. First, you have to decide whether to answer the question or whether to ask a question about it. If the interviewer asks, for example, "Tell me about your background," you can ask, "Would you like me to start with my education or my work experience?" On the other hand, you can use that opportunity to point out your strengths, knowledge of the job, and information about the company.

As soon as you have made the choice to answer the question, you have to decide where to begin. As often as possible, try to use general questions to give the information you decided you wanted to communicate in your analysis of strengths. Of course, if a question is really vague and you have no idea what the interviewer means, ask for clarification.

When you are asked a problem-solving question, the first thing to do is think. Don't be afraid to take some time to plan your answer. The interviewer will respect you more. Try to hear the entire problem when it is first presented, but if it is complicated and you have missed some part, ask to have it repeated.

Answer as if you are already on the job. Don't speak as if you are a student but as if you are already a worker. Remember that you will be part of an organization. One of the key questions in the interviewer's mind is: "Do I want this person on my team?" While you do not want to go running to your boss too quickly, you also do not want to seem to be taking on the whole world by yourself.

Remember your strengths that you identified on the worksheets in this chapter. Remember how they match the skills and knowledge this job requires. Use that information in answering any type of question.

You also identified weaknesses on your worksheets. Understanding your own weaknesses will help you with your answers when one of them is brought up in an interview. It is important that you be honest about your background, but do not make it seem worse than it really is. Suppose you dropped out of high school, have just completed your equivalency diploma, and are now in a job interview. You do not have to walk in and say, "I dropped out of high school for three years. That's it. Take it or leave it." However, if the interviewer asks about your education, you can say something like the following:

> I have just completed my equivalency diploma. Maybe I should have stayed in high school, but it wasn't right for me at the time. As I got older and smarter, I realized I did need more education. In fact, now that I have my diploma, I am planning to take some courses at the community college at night.

Questions you need not answer

Federal and state laws prohibit employers from asking certain questions unless they are directly related to the job for which you are being interviewed. The areas of your life about which you cannot be questioned include the following:

Questions about your race, religion, or ethnic origin

Questions about your marital status or children

Questions about your age, height, weight, health, or handicapping conditions

Questions about whom you date or live with or about your friends

You are permitted by law to answer these questions, but the employer is not allowed to ask them. Before you decide to answer them, think about how you would feel working for an employer who asks these kinds of questions. You may think the employer is asking them because he or she does not know they are illegal. However, so much has been written about them that it is hard to believe an employer would not know the rules.

You may decide to answer briefly and then say, "I think there are more important things about me that relate to this job. I would rather talk about them." Of course, if you refuse to answer, you might not get the job. This in itself is discrimination. If you think you have been discriminated against on an illegal basis, you can file a complaint with the Equal Employment Opportunity Commission in Washington, D.C. You can contact the Fair Employment Practices Commission in your own state and decide whether filing a complaint with them is appropriate. And you can also sue the company, using your own attorney.

Of course, you should not go into an interview expecting to be asked inappropriate questions. Most employers are familiar with the laws and abide by them. If you begin with suspicions, you may divert yourself from your real purpose—getting a job.

Listening—A Special Tip

Listening is the key to winning answers and to a winning interview. You let people know you are listening to them by facing them and by maintaining eye contact.

One of the most important reasons for listening to the interviewer is so that you can hear the question. People who don't listen, who are jumping ahead in their minds to answer questions they have not yet heard, do not do well in interviews. Not only do they fail to provide the information requested, but they come across as poor communicators, as being "out of it."

A major part of listening is not interrupting. Sometimes it is hard to tell if the interviewer has finished speaking or is just pausing to gather thoughts or breathe. Generally speaking, you can tell by watching the person. If the interviewer turns to you or looks at you, a response is probably called for. On the other hand, if the interviewer is looking into the distance or down at the desk, it is probably just a pause in speech.

Remember that one of *The 7 Habits of Highly Effective People* is to "seek first to understand, then to be understood." Good listening is the secret of understanding.

Summary Worksheet

This chapter took you through seven steps to a winning interview. Look over the checklist below to be sure you have worked on all parts of the seven steps.

_____ I have sheets prepared to make appointments for interviews, and I know what information I need.

_____ I have thought about my strengths and my weaknesses.

_____ I understand the requirements of the job or jobs I am looking for.

_____ I know how my skills and knowledge meet the job requirements.

_____ I know how to discuss my weaknesses or limitations.

_____ I know how I want to look on the day of a job interview.

_____ I have cleaned and prepared the clothes I will wear.

_____ I know how to use my nervous energy.

_____ I know the kinds of questions to expect and some ways to answer them.

_____ I am prepared to listen before I answer.

KEEPING YOUR JOB

Section II

Hired!—Finding Out the Facts

You've done it! You've received a job offer. Now you want to be sure that you will be successful on your first job. One of the keys to success is knowing that you are in the right job. The first part of this chapter is about questions you will be sure you want answered *before* you accept the job.

Once you are on the job, there is more basic information that you need, information about your responsibilities and your rewards and how the company or organization works, and information about key people. This chapter is designed to help you find and organize that information so that you can fit in easily to your new job.

Should I Accept
this Job?

During the interview, the employer had the opportunity to ask you questions about yourself. In a sense, at that point you were the seller, selling your services, and the employer was the buyer, deciding whether you have the services the company needs. Once the employer offers you a job, the focus changes. Now it is up to you to be sure that you want to accept the job.

In order to make the decision about whether or not you want a particular job, you have to think ahead of time about what you expect from a job. You have already made a choice about the type of work you will do by the kinds of jobs for which you are applying. However, there are often differences in what different companies or organizations offer to their employees, as well as differences in what they expect from them. Seven important ways in which particular jobs or companies can differ follow. As you look at this list, you will see that there is no such thing as a good or bad company. What appeals to one worker may not be desirable to another. Think about what appeals to you.

Seven areas to consider before accepting a job

1. *Work schedule.* Are the hours regular or irregular? Is evening or weekend work expected? Is there overtime?

2. *Work setting.* Is most of the work indoors in an office, store, factory, or shop? Is most of the work outdoors? Is it a combination of the two?

3. *Travel.* Does this job require local travel, travel within the city or nearby areas? Does this job require out-of-town travel?

4. *Salary.* What salary is being paid for this job? Is the salary determined on an annual, monthly, weekly, or hourly basis?

5. *Benefits.* What additional benefits are offered? Is health insurance paid for by the company? Is there reimbursement for additional education?

6. *Advancement.* Are there possibilities for moving up within this organization or will I have to move out to move up?

7. *Permanence.* Is this job temporary or "permanent"? (There is no such thing as a *truly* permanent job, but some jobs start out as temporary. They often provide a good way to get beginning experience.) Am I on the staff, working on a contract, or is the work seasonal with layoffs during slow periods?

Once you have decided upon the areas that are important to you, you are ready to ask questions *after* you have been offered the job.

Remember, until you have been offered that job, you are the seller. Before you talk about price, you want to convince the employer that you are the best possible person for the job. Many employers when interviewed said that the worst thing a person could do was to sound as if he or she just wanted the most money for the least amount of work. Of course, you do want the best possible salary for the work you do, but the important thing in the interview is to communicate how important the actual work is to you. Sometimes during the interview, you will be asked if you have any questions. A good question to ask is: "What will be the major responsibilities of this job?"

On the next page, you will find a Job Offer Worksheet. It lists many questions you can ask an employer once you have been offered the job. Look over the Job Offer Worksheet. Put a check next to each question that is important to you. Then fill in your ideal (but realistic) answer, the answer that would make you say, "Yes, this job is for me." When you have been offered a job, ask the questions that are important to you. Finally, compare the employer's answers with your ideal answers. You have to remember that no job is perfect. What you will be looking for in an actual job offer is the best possible combination of your ideals and the company's reality.

You may want to make copies of this worksheet so that you can use it for more than one offer.

Job Offer Worksheet

_____ 1. What is my starting salary?

Your Desire _____

Actual Offer _____

_____ 2. What are the hours and days of work?

Your Desire _____

Actual Offer _____

_____ 3. Is there overtime work?

Your Desire _____

Actual Offer _____

_____ 4. How will I be paid for overtime? extra pay? time off?

Your Desire _____

Actual Offer _____

_____ 5. How are salary increases determined?

Your Desire _____

Actual Offer _____

_____ 6. What kind of health insurance plan will I get?

Your Desire _____

Actual Offer _____

_____ 7. Who pays for the health insurance?

Your Desire _____

Actual Offer _____

_____ 8. Is there any reimbursement for college, graduate school, or other training?

Your Desire _____

Actual Offer _____

_____ 9. Is there any local or out-of-town travel?

Your Desire _____

Actual Offer _____

_____ 10. How will I be reimbursed for work-related travel expenses?

Your Desire _____

Actual Offer _____

_____11. How many vacation days do I get a year?

        Your Desire _____

        Actual Offer _____

_____12. What restrictions are there, if any, on taking vacations?

        Your Desire _____

        Actual Offer _____

_____13. What is the organization's sick leave policy?

        Your Desire _____

        Actual Offer _____

_____14. Is there a union I must join?

        Your Desire _____

        Actual Offer _____

The First Days— Fitting in Easily

Some large companies provide an orientation to all new employees on one of the first days they work. The purpose of an orientation is to get you started with all the facts you need about the company and your job. Orienting someone means pointing that person in the right direction. Whether or not your company does this, there is essential information you will want to get so you can move in the right direction. This information will make you more comfortable on the job and make you a more valuable employee. It will also help you begin to get ahead as soon as you get there.

Your first job may be in a factory, an office, a store, a hospital, or any one of dozens of other settings. Some of the information you need will vary with the kind of job you have, but some of it is basic. Sometimes all you need to know can seem overwhelming, but if it is broken down into smaller parts, you can see that some of the information you will find out very easily just in the course of events. You may want to ask your immediate supervisor for some of the information. Other information you will get from your co-workers. Some information will come to you through your own observations.

In the pages that follow, there are ten worksheets that deal with different times and aspects of the workday. They begin with your arrival and end with your leaving at the close of a workday. In between, they deal with such things as key people, getting supplies, and taking lunch. Look all of them over. Select the ones that have meaning for you in the job you have accepted or expect to take. Once on the job, find out the answers to the questions that apply to you.

Orientation Worksheet 1—Arrival

The information on this worksheet will help you get off to a good start every day.

1. What time am I expected at work?

_____

2. How does anyone know I am there? Do I punch a time clock?

_____

3. At what time is the office or shop unlocked?

_____
_____
_____
_____

4. What do I do if I get there and it's locked?

_____
_____

5. Where do I get the tools or supplies I need to start work each day?

_____
_____
_____
_____
_____
_____
_____

6. Exactly where do I report?

_____
_____
_____
_____
_____
_____
_____
_____

Orientation Worksheet 2—Key People

It is very important that you learn the names of people as quickly as possible. If you are in an office, one of the good ways to do this is to keep an index card on your desk and just jot down the names of people as you meet them, with some way for you to remember who they are. Eventually you will not need that help. You will know all the people who will be important in your work life.

1. What is the name of my immediate supervisor?

_____

_____

_____

2. How do I see that person? Is he or she right there? Do I telephone? Do I need an appointment?

_____

_____

_____

3. What is the name of the president of the company? the head of the division in which I am working?

_____

_____

_____

_____

4. What are the names of the co-workers who are working closest to me?

_____

_____

_____

_____

_____

5. Who are the other people I have identified as important in the organization or in my work?

_____

_____

_____

_____

_____

_____

Orientation Worksheet 3—Responsibilities

This worksheet is important to every worker, new and experienced. There is no job without responsibilities.

1. What tasks am I supposed to do?

_____

_____

_____

_____

_____

_____

_____

2. Am I supposed to get started by myself or wait for instructions?

_____

_____

_____

_____

_____

_____

_____

3. Who gives me instructions?

_____

_____

_____

_____

_____

4. What do I do when I have finished the work I was asked to do?

_____

_____

_____

_____

_____

Orientation Worksheet 4—Tools, Equipment, and Supplies

This worksheet is particularly important if you are working in a job where you need to use a lot of objects.

1. What are the major tools or supplies I need?

_____

_____

_____

_____

_____

_____

2. Who is responsible for supplying them?

_____

_____

_____

_____

3. Where do I get supplies? Is there any procedure for requesting them or signing them out?

_____

_____

_____

_____

4. What do I do if a piece of equipment is not working?

_____

_____

_____

_____

5. If I am asked to lay out money to buy something for the office or shop, or to go somewhere, how do I get it back?

_____

_____

_____

_____

Orientation Worksheet 5—Dealing with the Public

In some jobs, most of the work involves dealing with the public, that is, with people outside the company. Often these are the customers or clients of the company. Most of these questions are for people working in sales.

1. To what extent am I supposed to deal with customers or clients?

_____

_____

_____

_____

_____

_____

2. How do I handle cash payments from customers?

_____

_____

_____

_____

_____

_____

3. How do I handle charge payments from customers?

_____

_____

_____

_____

_____

_____

4. What is the company policy on complaints?

_____

_____

_____

_____

_____

_____

Orientation Worksheet 6—Lunch and Other Breaks

Use this worksheet to help you figure out company policy on lunch and other breaks, as well as things you can do during those periods to relax and enjoy your time.

1. How much time is allowed for lunch?

_____

2. Is there some particular schedule I must follow when I take lunch?

_____

3. Is there a company cafeteria where I can buy food or a company lunchroom where I can bring food and eat in?

_____

4. What are some of the good and inexpensive eating places nearby?

_____

_____

_____

_____

_____

5. If I bring lunch from home, is there a refrigerator I can use?

_____

6. Are there some interesting places to walk during lunch?

_____

_____

_____

_____

7. Are there any other scheduled breaks?

_____

_____

_____

_____

_____

8. Where are the restrooms? Do I need a key?

_____

Orientation Worksheet 7—Getting Paid

This worksheet will help you understand your paycheck and be sure that it is correct. You should know your salary when you are hired. However, your gross salary is not the same as your net salary. Your gross salary is the amount the employer is paying for your work. Then deductions are made for federal, state, and sometimes local taxes and for social security. There may be other deductions for health insurance and union dues. On some of these you may have a choice. What is left after deductions is your net pay.

1. When am I paid?

_____

2. What will my gross salary each pay period be?

_____

3. Am I being paid on an hourly basis, in which the pay will be different each pay period based on the number of hours I worked, or am I being paid the same amount each pay period?

_____

4. If I am being paid on an hourly basis, how is my pay figured?

_____

_____

5. What deductions, besides tax and social security, will there be and how much will each one be?

_____

_____

_____

6. If I am entitled to overtime pay, when will I receive it?

_____

_____

Orientation Worksheet 8—Unions

Some jobs and some companies are unionized; that is, a union has won the right to carry out collective bargaining on behalf of the workers—that's you.

There are four types of memberships. Where there is an *open shop*, you will find union and nonunion workers employed side by side. You are free to join or not to join. Where there is an *agency shop*, you will also find union and nonunion people working together. However, everyone must pay an agency fee to the union. You may decide to join or not to join. If you join, you will pay somewhat more than the agency fee, and you will get additional benefits. Where there is a *union shop*, all employees must become union members once they get the job. You will have no choice about joining. Where there is a *closed shop*, you must be a member of the union before you get the job. If you have gotten the job, you are already a member.

1. Is there a union?

_____

2. What type of shop is it?

_____

3. What are the benefits of union membership?

_____

_____

_____

4. What is the cost of union membership?

_____

5. Who is my union representative?

_____

Orientation Worksheet 9—Getting Sick and Staying Well

No one plans to get sick, but unfortunately most of us do find ourselves with a cold or the flu from time to time. While employers expect you to be on the job regularly, no one wants you to come to work if you are too sick to perform your job. It is important that you call as soon as you know you are not going to be able to come to work. You should make the call yourself, unless you are really too sick to do so. Having someone else call for you does not convince your employer that you are sick, and it does not give the employer the chance to ask you any questions about the work you have been doing.

1. What is the company policy on sick leave?

_____

2. If I am sick, whom should I call?

_____

3. What is that person's or office's telephone number and extension?

_____

4. When I return, is there any special procedure to follow?

_____

_____

5. How do I report sick days on the time clock or time report sheets?

_____

_____

6. Does my company offer any health maintenance or fitness services?

_____

_____

Orientation Worksheet 10—End of the Day

Just as you want to arrive on time and make a good first impression, it is important to learn not only the company rules but the customs for the end of the day.

1. At what time do I officially finish work?

_____

_____

_____

2. If I am in the middle of a job, what am I expected to do?

_____

_____

_____

3. Am I supposed to wait for someone to take over my work, to relieve me?

_____

_____

_____

4. Whose job is it to turn off any equipment at the end of the day?

_____

_____

_____

5. Whose job is it to lock away valuable items?

_____

_____

_____

6. Is there a safe place to leave my tools?

_____

_____

_____

7. Whose job is it to close the office or lock the shop at the end of the day?

_____

_____

_____

Summary Worksheet

In this chapter you figured out the information you will want to have before you accept a job and the information you need once you are on the job. Probably there was information suggested in the chapter that did not interest you or that did not have anything to do with your work. You also learned how to sort out the information that is important to you from all the kinds of information listed. Use the checklist below to confirm your thinking.

_____I know what is important to me in looking for a job.

_____I know not to introduce questions of salary and hours until after I have been offered a job.

_____I have thought about what it means to orient myself to a job, to point myself in the right direction.

_____I have looked over all the orientation worksheets and picked out the questions that have meaning for me.

_____I know how to begin the day.

_____I know how to deal with customers or clients.

_____I know the names of the people who are important to me in the organization.

_____I know how to find or store tools and supplies.

_____I know about lunch and other breaks.

_____I know what to do if I will be sick and unable to work.

_____I know how to end the day.

On-the-Job Success

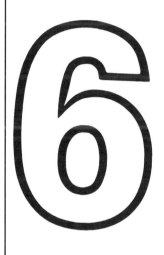

Now that you are on the job and have mastered the basics that you need to know, you want to be sure that you know what behaviors will bring success. Whether you want to keep this job, get promoted within the organization, or find a different job somewhere else, a key to your future success is your present success.

In the first section of this book, you took a look at the habits and skills of success and saw how those applied to getting a job. Now you can examine what it takes to be successful once the job is yours. A large part of being successful rests in recognizing our interdependence with other people. Interdependence does not mean that we depend or lean on others for help. It also doesn't mean that it's our job to give help to others. Interdependence is bigger than either of these ideas. It means we cannot function at all without each other.

Necessary Skills for On-the-Job Success

The United States Department of Labor has been studying the nature of on-the-job success. It has reported its findings and conclusions in a booklet, *What Work Requires of School: A SCANS Report for America 2000.* The word *SCANS* in the title stands for the Secretary's Commission on Achieving Necessary Skills. It is the *necessary skills* part that is of greatest interest to us. Whether you learn these skills in school or on your own, they are the skills that employers want in their employees—that's you—in order to have successful, competitive businesses. Just as a business can get ahead by having employees with these skills, you can be successful by being an employee who has them.

Before we get to the skills themselves, we need to understand two more things. First, these skills are different from the technical knowledge that you may need on the job. Of course, a word-processing machine operator must know how to type and use software, and a salesperson must know the product, the prices, and how to persuade people to buy. But they both need particular personal and interpersonal competencies to use their knowledge in effective ways. The second important idea is that the skills were identified nationwide as being important. So you can be sure that they are important to employers in your community, whether you live in a large city, a suburb, or a farming area.

The necessary skills are built on a three-part foundation. The first part of the foundation is the *basic skills.* The basic skills include reading, writing, arithmetic, listening, and speaking. The second part of the foundation is *thinking skills.* Thinking skills include decision making, problem solving, reasoning, and knowing how to learn. But the area of skills most related to this section of the book is the area of *personal skills.* There are five personal skills listed in the SCANS Report. They are as follows:

1. Responsibility—You work hard toward reaching a goal.

2. Self-esteem—You believe in your own self-worth.

3. Sociability—You show understanding of others and act with politeness in group settings.

4. Self-management—You set your own goals, measure your own progress, and show self-control.

5. Integrity/Honesty—You choose the ethical course of action.

In addition to the basic skills, the report identifies competencies—things every worker should be able to do. Eight of these competencies are very important to you as a beginning worker. It will not surprise you by now to learn that one of the main areas of competency is in the "interpersonal" area. Here are the eight competencies. Mastering the first four will bring you a long way toward satisfying the overall goal of working well with others.

1. You work well as a member of a team and you contribute to the group effort.

2. You know how to serve clients or customers.

3. You are willing to negotiate to help resolve differences of opinion or of interests.

4. You work well with men and women from diverse backgrounds.

5. You know how to allocate your time and follow schedules to meet the goals of your work.

6. You know how to acquire, store, and use materials efficiently.

7. You can acquire, evaluate, and maintain up-to-date information.

8. You know how to choose appropriate procedures, tools, or equipment.

Of course, you are not expected to memorize these lists. The important thing is not that there are five of one kind of skill and eight of another. The important thing is for each of us to learn how to get the best from ourselves and how to work well with others. The suggestions and the worksheets in the previous chapter helped you gather information you need to get off to a good start on the job. This chapter gives you food for thought on working with others, including bosses, customers, co-workers and people who may report to you.

A checklist of skills   Take a look at the checklist that follows. It is similar to the one you completed at the end of the first chapter. These items are also drawn from "The National Career Development Guidelines" of the National Occupational Information Coordinating Committee. Use it as you did the first one, to identify your current strengths and to double-check when you complete this section of the book, to see what you have learned.

READY TO KEEP A JOB
A Checklist of Indicators

Directions: In the first column, place a check next to those job-seeking skills you think you have "NOW." Place a question mark next to the ones you would like to find out more about. If you are uncertain, leave the space blank. As you read through this book, come back and place a plus sign in the second column, "LATER," when you think you have really mastered a particular skill.

NOW   LATER   ESSENTIAL SKILLS FOR JOB SEEKING

____   ____   1. Demonstrate interpersonal skills required for working with, and for, others.

____   ____   2. Describe appropriate employer and employee interactions in various situations.

____   ____   3. Demonstrate how to express feelings, reactions, and ideas, in an appropriate manner.

____   ____   4. Describe healthy ways of dealing with stress.

____   ____   5. Demonstrate positive work attitudes and behaviors.

____   ____   6. Demonstrate a realistic understanding of self.

____   ____   7. Demonstrate behaviors, attitudes, and skills that work to eliminate stereotyping in education, family, and work environments.

____   ____   8. Describe how family and leisure functions affect occupational roles and decisions.

____   ____   9. Demonstrate confidence in the ability to learn new things.

____   ____   10. Describe community and organizational resources that support education and training.

What Employers Want

Some people find it hard to understand what an employer is looking for and why he or she prefers one employee over another. They think the employer is just playing favorites or that the employee is just bending over backwards to be liked, trying to be the "teacher's pet." Well, work is not like school. In school, teachers do have to try to be fair to everyone. At work, employers try to identify the best employees because better workers mean a more successful business operation. The best workers get the rewards of promotions and raises.

Research with employers and with recently hired employees reveals what employers are looking for and what most workers need to learn if they are to be successful. This chapter will let you in on the findings of the research and present you with situations or case studies to help you see things from both the worker's and the employer's points of view.

In general, research about what makes a worker successful, what can make you successful on the job, focuses on attitude. Before you are hired, the boss can find out if you really know how to type or if you have learned how to replace brakes. He or she cannot know how you will behave with other people while you are doing it. Your boss cannot know whether you will work hard or look for the easiest way out. He or she cannot know whether you will come to work late and be absent frequently, or whether you can be depended upon to be there.

There are ten skills for success that we will focus on in this chapter. These skills were drawn from several studies conducted with employers in a wide range of industries in different parts of the United States, as well as from the SCANS Report mentioned in the last chapter. Knowing something about these studies may help you see how similar employers are in their desires for the ideal or best possible employee.

"Termination is usually the result of poor use of time, poor attendance, and poor attitude rather than the result of incompetence." This was one of the key findings of a study conducted among employers of two vocational training institutions' graduates in Wisconsin. The same study found that, "demonstrating a willingness to learn, being punctual and regular in attendance, and keeping supervisors informed are important for the new worker."

Lack of responsibility, lack of initiative, and absenteeism were the three most troublesome problems with beginning workers, according to employers of beginning office workers. This study was conducted in the state of

New York and included businesses in both New York City and the rural areas of the state.

Efficiency, courtesy, pride, and enthusiasm in one's work were found to be the most important worker qualities in a study of more than two hundred businesses in New Hampshire.

"Employers find that most job applicants are not lacking as much in knowing how to do the job, the technical skills, as they are in attitude toward work and the ability to communicate with and relate to others." This was the finding of a three-year study that included employers of clerical workers, data processors, and word-processing machine operators; computer specialists; freight and traffic handlers; salespeople; workers in international trade; social service workers; people in audio-visual, printing, and energy industry occupations; and many others.

In another study in New York City, employers of recent high school graduates were asked to rank fourteen worker traits that had already been identified as important on-the-job qualities. The employers ranked the following three traits highest:

1. Follows through on a job assignment

2. Is a productive worker

3. Comes to work regularly

If you look over the ten Orientation Worksheets in the chapter before this one, you will see how you are already beginning to identify and exhibit some of the skills for success identified in the studies. Getting information is part of adapting to an organization. Certainly you cannot get to work on time if you don't know what time you are expected, and you cannot let your supervisor know what you are doing if you don't know who your supervisor is. Now it is time to zero in on the ten skills for success. Each of the skills is discussed in the pages that follow, with examples from both the employer's and employee's points of view.

Ten skills for success

1. Be dependable—give a full day's work.

2. Work well with your supervisor.

3. Know when to ask questions.

4. Cooperate with co-workers.

5. Carry out your responsibilities.

6. Take pride in what you do.

7. Show initiative—learn new skills, take on new tasks.

8. Look your best.

9. Control your emotions.

10. Become a part of the organization.

Be Dependable—Give a Full Day's Work

How boring. It seems as if all of your life people have been telling you to be on time. Teachers were always saying terrible things would happen if you were late to school. But when you were late, what happened? You got a late pass. Well, maybe your grades would have been better if you had gotten there. That all seems unimportant now.

A job is different. You really need to get there on time because the company or organization is waiting for you to perform your work. Unlike school, where each person's work is separate from every other person's, wherever you are working there is a chain of work in which one person's successful performance depends upon another's.

Imagine you are a typist in an office. Your supervisor, Mr. McNeill, has to give a report to the president of the company, Ms. Chase. Mr. McNeill spent most of last night writing the report. He is waiting for you to type it. Ms. Chase is waiting to receive it. Imagine how Mr. McNeill feels when you walk in a few minutes early ready to work. Imagine how he feels if you get there half an hour late.

Now picture yourself as a general worker in a local hardware and locksmith shop. Your boss, Mr. Folger, opens the shop at 7:30 in the morning. He immediately gets a call from Ms. Elson who says that he must come to help her fix the broken lock on her front door. She cannot leave. She cannot take her children to school or get to work herself because the door will be wide open. Mr. Folger assures Ms. Elson that he will be there at 8:15, since he knows you get in at 8:00 and can take over in the shop. Imagine how Mr. Folger feels when he sees you walk in at 7:45. Imagine how he feels when you walk in at 8:20.

You need to be on time so that you are a strong link in the chain of work. You want to be on time for another reason. Many of the skills for success that we will be discussing in this chapter are hard to assess. It is very easy, on the other hand, to see if someone is there or not there. Often supervisors and employers are willing to give a new worker a chance to work out. They don't jump on every little mistake. They are patient. However, if they get to the point where they are about to give up on you, your not being where you are supposed to be is often the final straw.

Being dependable means not only getting to work on time but being on the job. That means taking no more time for lunch than you are entitled to and not goofing off. Some people get to work all right. Then they spend a lot of time, more than they need, in the restroom or visiting with co-workers. Other people never seem to get back from some errand outside the office as quickly as most people do. All of these undependable behaviors mean that your employer is not getting a full day's work for the money being paid you. No one wants to be cheated.

Situation Study 1

Alice Edwards had found the job she wanted. She was going to work as a typist in an insurance company, and she had the chance to attend classes to learn the latest in word processing.

The first day was fine. She was expected at work at 9:00 A.M. She was happy to see that she got to the building just on time. She had a little trouble finding the right office, but she was there before 9:30, and her new boss, Audrey Russell, was very sympathetic about her getting lost in the building.

After two months, Alice felt she was doing very well on the job. She had improved her typing skills and was scheduled to begin word-processing training in a few weeks. She had missed the first training session because she had to leave early every day for a week to go to the dentist. Ms. Russell had said she could do it but hadn't looked very happy about it. But what could Alice do? She had always gone to the dentist in October.

Alice was quite surprised to be called into her boss's office that morning. It was 9:30, and Ms. Russell was waiting for her at her desk when she arrived. Ms. Russell said that Alice kept coming late and had missed time for the dentist and that this had to be improved or Alice would be fired! Alice explained that the bus she took left her off on the corner just at 9:00, and that meant she was just a little late each day. The next earlier bus would mean that Alice would have to leave her house forty-five minutes earlier. Audrey Russell seemed not to care and repeated that Alice would be fired if she kept missing work.

Imagine you are Alice Edwards.

How do you feel?

_____

_____

_____

_____

_____

_____

_____

_____

What will you do?

_____

_____

_____

_____

_____

_____

_____

_____

Imagine you are Audrey Russell.

How do you feel?

_____
_____
_____
_____
_____
_____
_____
_____
_____
_____
_____
_____
_____
_____
_____
_____

What will you do?

_____
_____
_____
_____
_____
_____
_____
_____
_____
_____
_____
_____
_____
_____
_____
_____
_____

(Hint: **Better late than never may soon become never.)**

Work Well with Your
Supervisor

Once you accept a job, your supervisor or boss becomes a key person in your life. You may be one of many people that person supervises, or you may be her or his entire staff. Some people are very good at being supervisors. They know how to help the people working for them so that they bring out the best in all workers. Some supervisors are patient and fair with everyone. It is a good idea to expect behavior like that from your supervisor. However, sometimes you will not be so lucky, and your supervisor will be more difficult to get along with. It is your job to adapt to your supervisor.

One of the skills you can use to get along with your boss is the skill of listening. This skill was discussed at the end of the chapter on interviewing. Remember to look at the person who is speaking to you and to pay attention to what that person is saying. Your boss will be giving you directions on what is expected of you and how to carry out your responsibilities. You cannot carry them out well if you have not heard them.

It is not a good idea to argue with your boss frequently, at least not when you are new on the job. You may think of ways you would prefer doing things over the ways that are explained. Maybe you learned some different techniques in school or on a part-time job. When you are new on a job, do things the way you are asked to do them. There is probably a reason that they are being done in a particular way. Sometimes the reason is not apparent. It may be because that is how the company has always done it. It may be that it is being done that way because it protects someone else who cannot do a particular task well. It may even be because it is the best way to do it. In the beginning, assume that the way you are being told is the right way. Then watch for a while and see if what you think is a better way would be an improvement. If you still think so, suggest it.

One newly employed worker, Jeff, was having a lot of trouble getting along with his boss, Mr. Sharp. Finally, Jeff figured out one of the problems. He realized that in school, teachers always had to listen to his ideas. That was their job—to help him figure out ideas and then to listen to them. While Mr. Sharp did have to teach him what to do, he did not have to listen to his ideas, nor did he want to.

Part of getting along with your supervisor is being able to accept constructive criticism. From your boss's point of view, all criticism is constructive. You are being criticized to improve your performance so that its contribution to the product or service of your organization will be better. Again, listening is the first step. Following through and making changes in how you do things is the second step. This does not mean that you should never question anything or make any suggestions. It does mean that it takes some time to get to know how and why things are done in an organization, and you need to be accepting for a while before presenting your opinion.

If you find you disagree with your supervisor, it is never a good idea to express this disagreement while you are being criticized. It is better to listen, think about the criticism, and then if you disagree with part of it say something like, "I have been thinking about your suggestion that I do A before B and then do C. It seems to me that I might save time if I did A first, then B and C together. What do you think?"

Loyalty to the organization is considered very important by most employers. You might wonder, especially if you are working in a large corporation, how you can show you are loyal to some product or service that is far removed from you. One of the ways is by being loyal to your supervisor. It is not a good idea to spend a lot of time criticizing your supervisor even when other people are griping. It is an even worse idea to do this with people in other divisions or units of the same organization. Work places are often big rumor mills. Until you make some friends you know you can trust, the best way to air your feelings about people at work is to talk to people who don't know them—people at home.

Going to your boss's supervisor to complain about something or someone, particularly about your boss, rarely works to your advantage. Sometimes when you are hired, you know someone higher up in the organization than your immediate supervisor. You will have to work extra hard in that case to convince your supervisor that you are loyal. If you go over your boss's head, her or his supervisor may very well interpret that as disloyalty and act to protect your boss, not you.

Go over your boss's head only if what you are trying to accomplish is very important to you; you have explored every other way to accomplish your goal; and you are willing to lose a great deal, perhaps even your job.

Situation Study 2

Frank Green was hired by a large corporation to work in the customer relations division. One of his tasks was dealing with customers when they had complaints. Another was setting up training sessions for salespeople.

Evelyn Harrod, Frank's supervisor, at first thought that Frank was going to work out very well. He was very patient with customers and was able to handle their complaints well. Ms. Harrod had only one complaint. Sometimes Mr. Green went so out of his way to help customers that he could not get enough of his other work done. She explained this to him, but he said, "Don't you want me to satisfy the customers?" She tried to explain about limiting his time with each customer. Frank said, "I just have to take the amount of time it takes to make each one really feel good."

When the time for the first training meeting came, Ms. Harrod asked Mr. Green to prepare a package of materials for each salesperson.

When the day of the training arrived, Ms. Harrod saw that instead of preparing one package of twelve items for each person, there were twelve stacks of papers and each person would have to be asked to take one. She felt this would take unnecessary time and she could not be sure each person had all of the materials. In addition, it seemed to indicate a poorly planned meeting, one that would not get off to a good, crisp start.

At the end of the meeting, she spoke to Mr. Green about not following her instructions. He said, "I didn't think it mattered, and I didn't have time to do it your way. They got all the material, didn't they?"

Imagine you are Frank Green.

How do you feel?

_____

_____

_____

_____

_____

_____

_____

What will you do?

_____

_____

_____

_____

_____

_____

_____

Imagine you are Evelyn Harrod.

How do you feel?

_____
_____
_____
_____
_____
_____
_____
_____
_____
_____
_____
_____
_____
_____
_____
_____

What will you do?

_____
_____
_____
_____
_____
_____
_____
_____
_____
_____
_____
_____
_____
_____
_____
_____
_____
_____

(*Hint:*   **Your time is my time.**)

Know When to Ask Questions

Part of getting along with your supervisor is knowing when and how to ask questions. Some supervisors like to structure everything and will welcome many questions from you. Others would prefer that you act more on your own. You will have to feel your way. However, there are two good basic rules:

1. If you really don't know how to do something, ask.

2. If you know the answer, don't ask.

Some people ask questions as a way of challenging their bosses. Those are questions like, "Are you sure you want me to do it *that* way?" or "Wouldn't you like me to try to do this the other way?" Those are generally not effective ways of presenting an opinion. If you want to suggest a change, wait until you are sure of yourself, then make the suggestion clearly. "I see another way to do that. I would like to describe it to you. When would be a good time?"

In general, when you are a new worker, it is better to ask questions about how to do something than not to ask. When you ask a question, be ready for the answer. Listen to the answer so you won't have to ask the same question again. Ask the question with a paper and pencil handy so that you can jot down the details of the answer.

Cooperate with Co-Workers

Just as you need to get along with your boss, you need to find ways of working with your co-workers, the people around you. This is important for several reasons. First of all, it is important to you. Getting along with the people around you will make your day easier and more pleasant. Experienced workers around you can often show you the ropes and help you figure out how things get done in your organization.

Getting along with your co-workers is also important to the company. In talking about the first success skill, dependability, we talked about the chain of work. In addition, there is a concept called team effort. Many jobs require several people working alongside each other for completion. If you are working on an assembly line, you can picture how each person's completion of a job leads to the next person's work. Now picture a situation like working in a hospital. The doctors, nurses, aides, and technicians of various kinds all work to help one patient. Both a chain of work and teamwork are needed.

In addition to the need for teamwork, better work is done when people feel good about their relationships with each other. If people feel they have no friends, that everyone around them is hostile and an enemy, then too much time is spent watching one's back rather than working.

This does not mean you have to accept everyone as your great buddy from the first day you are at work. In most places, someone will ask you to have lunch or will walk with you as you leave. Be open to friendly gestures. Listen to people. Choose friends at work as you would choose them elsewhere. However, don't divide your co-workers into mental lists of friends and enemies. Most will not be either. They will simply be your co-workers.

There are two kinds of behavior that really turn people off at work. One is not doing your share of the work. The other is being a know-it-all. You can avoid the first by doing your work. You can avoid the second by staying out of other people's work and by not talking about all you know, especially about things that are not your job.

Situation Study 3

Barbara Masters had been hired to do the billing for a large mail order company. Jerry Noff, her boss, had explained that things were really in a mess because the previous bookkeeper had not known what he was doing. Barbara felt she could do the work and was glad to get a first job that had a challenge to it.

When Barbara got the records that had to be corrected and had to result in actual bills, she saw that it was even worse than Mr. Noff had said. She looked things over and saw a way to do it that she thought was better. Barbara explained her method to Mr. Noff, and he said, "Ms. Masters, I would appreciate anything you can do to straighten this out as quickly as possible. It sounds like you know what you're talking about. Go right ahead."

Barbara got to work, and her method was working. But the work was tedious and time-consuming. She had to look at all these poorly written records. She decided she had to take a break, so she walked away from her desk for a few minutes to Mary Harris, whom she'd met at lunch.

Mary was working on a microcomputer. Barbara knew a lot about computers. She had taken computer courses and liked to fool around with programming. Barbara watched Mary for a few minutes. She was working on a new record system that would include billing. Barbara realized that Mary was using the ABC software, when it was obvious that XYZ would be much better. "Wait a minute," Barbara said to Mary. "Why don't you switch to XYZ? You could write that program much more easily, and it could hold a lot more data."

Imagine you are Mary Harris.

How do you feel?

_____

_____

_____

_____

_____

_____

_____

_____

What will you do?

_____

_____

_____

_____

_____

_____

_____

_____

Imagine you are Barbara Masters.

How do you feel?

_____
_____
_____
_____
_____
_____
_____

What will you do?

_____
_____
_____
_____
_____
_____
_____

Imagine you are Jerry Noff.

How do you feel?

_____
_____
_____
_____
_____
_____
_____

What will you do?

_____
_____
_____
_____
_____
_____
_____

(*Hint:*   **Carry your own weight—not others'.**)

Carry Out Your Responsibilities

Every job has its responsibilities. These include the tasks you are expected to carry out and the methods you are supposed to use to carry them out. Responsibilities also include knowing how to take proper care of the tools, equipment, or supplies you use and following the work schedule that has been laid out for you. A person who carries out all of his or her responsibilities as expected is a person who can be trusted with more responsibilities. That person is considered trustworthy by the supervisor.

In the previous chapter, you used orientation worksheets to help identify your responsibilities. In Orientation Worksheet 3, you looked at your responsibilities. In Orientation Worksheet 4, you thought about tools, equipment, and supplies. It would be a good idea to look at those worksheets again now.

Once you know your responsibilities, it is up to you to carry them out. If you are avoiding some of them because you don't know how to do them, or you are afraid of not doing them well, it is a good idea to speak to your supervisor and get some help. It is better for you to admit you don't know something than to have your supervisor find out that you simply have not been doing it. The effect of your not carrying out your responsibilities goes beyond the poor impression it gives of you. It affects the chain of work and the teamwork of the organization.

There are a number of ways to demonstrate your trustworthiness. If you handle money—take cash for sales, get reimbursed for expenses, buy materials for the company—you must always be sure that your dealings are completely honest and that your records of these dealings are up-to-date and correct. If your schedule is flexible and sometimes your work is in the office and sometimes outside, it is a good idea to make sure that your supervisor knows where you are at all times.

Situation Study 4

Robert Broom was hired as a truck driver for a food company. His job was to drive the truck in the mornings on a set route, making deliveries to particular customers. While he was on his route in the morning, calls came from other customers for special deliveries to be made in the afternoon. Some afternoons there were a lot of deliveries, on others very few.

Robert liked his job. It gave him a chance to be outside, and he enjoyed driving. He liked the few minutes he had to chat with each customer. After a few weeks, he saw that by varying the route just a little, he could serve all the customers and end up in a different place for lunch every day. He didn't like the afternoons as much. If there were too few special deliveries, he just sat around in the office with nothing to do but wait.

Steven Peters was Robert's boss and the owner of the company. He liked Robert and thought he did a good job. He kept the truck nice and clean and was always there on time in the morning.

One day Steven got a call from an afternoon customer that was urgent. Steven needed to get to Robert in the middle of the morning so that Robert could interrupt his deliveries and serve this customer. Steven got out the schedule of deliveries and figured out where Robert would be at that time of the morning. He called; Robert had been there half an hour earlier. He called a place further down the list; Robert had been there first thing in the morning.

Steven never caught up with Robert. The customer was unreasonable and said he would never deal with them again. When Robert got back to the office, Steven was very angry. He asked Robert where he had been. When Robert told him about the route changes, Steven said that Robert should stick to the route he had given him or quit.

Imagine you are Robert Broom.

How do you feel?

_____
_____
_____

What will you do?

_____
_____
_____

Imagine you are Steven Peters.

How do you feel?

_____
_____
_____

What will you do?

_____
_____
_____

Take Pride in What You Do

The sixth skill for success is often called conscientiousness. People who have this skill take pride in what they do. They see what they are doing as important work. They see their work through to the finish and consider it a finished piece of work even when it is part of a much larger operation.

There is no work that is not important. Some work is necessary for people's basic needs and others for their desires. All of it contributes to the country's economic health. It is true that some jobs get higher pay and some jobs have more prestige, but the pride in one's own work has nothing to do with that.

Employers look for workers who set high performance standards for themselves and whose work is of a high quality, even when doing so means that the employee had to put in some extra time or effort.

Some people will say, "It's not my job," or "Why should I care? They're earning the big bucks." One reason to care is because it feels better. Another reason for you to care is because extra effort is a key to success. Now that you have your first job, watch the people in your organization who are successful. You will see that many of them do things that others should be doing for them, things that are not their job. One of the big differences between people who just get by and people who succeed is the willingness to go the extra mile, to pitch in and help.

In an office, being conscientious may mean cleaning the plate of the photocopying machine and rerunning copies when you see that what you have done is all full of gray smudges. In a shop, being conscientious may mean going for a replacement tool or part when you see that the one you have will work, but not perfectly. In a store, being conscientious may mean being the one who replaces the shopping bags when the supply at your station has been used up.

Situation Study 5

Leonard Anderson and Carrie Curran were both somewhat new workers in the company. Carrie had been there six months, Leonard three. Carrie was a secretary. Leonard was a sales representative.

The company was planning to announce a new product. Everyone was very excited about it. Ellen Brock, who was Leonard and Carrie's supervisor and the head of the division responsible for the product, saw this as a big chance for the division, for everyone in it, and for herself.

Small replicas of the product had been made for everyone who would attend the announcement. This included the company bigwigs, the stockholders, and some major customers. Ellen had worked very hard on a one-page description of how to use the product. This was to be given out along with the replicas.

Ellen asked Leonard and Carrie to see that the product and a copy of the report were on each of the two hundred seats. A half hour before the meeting, Ellen went in to check the room. Half the seats had the product. Half had the reports. All the reports were poor copies.

Ellen was very upset. She called Leonard and Carrie into her office. Leonard said, "We ran out of replicas, and it's not my job to look for more." Carrie said, "I know where the replicas are, but he didn't ask me." "What about the copies?" asked Ellen. "Well," answered Carrie, "the photocopying machine is broken so I couldn't finish them." "She could have taken them down to the third floor. There's a machine there," muttered Leonard.

Imagine you are Carrie Curran.

How do you feel?

_____

_____

_____

_____

_____

_____

_____

What will you do?

_____

_____

_____

_____

_____

_____

_____

_____

Imagine you are Leonard Anderson.

How do you feel?

_____
_____
_____
_____
_____
_____
_____

What will you do?

_____
_____
_____
_____
_____
_____
_____

Imagine you are Ellen Brock.

How do you feel?

_____
_____
_____
_____
_____
_____
_____

What will you do?

_____
_____
_____
_____
_____
_____
_____

Show Initiative—Learn New Skills, Take on New Tasks

Initiative is the big step beyond conscientiousness. Just as you want to do every job you are supposed to do to the best of your ability, you also want to look for opportunities to add responsibilities and learn new things.

In many organizations, promotion comes after you have earned it. This means that if you want to move up in a company, you often need to be willing to take on some new responsibilities before you are being paid to do so.

In earlier sections of this chapter, we stressed doing what you are told to do. That is good for the first few months on the job. After that, if you see a better way to do something that you think will be accepted, then you can suggest that to your boss. Some companies have suggestion boxes or formal ways of suggesting improvements.

Sometimes, you will have the opportunity to take on new responsibilities because some big job comes along and your organization is shorthanded. Sometimes the opportunity comes along because someone is away unexpectedly. Take these opportunities as soon as you feel you can carry them out well.

Some companies offer the opportunity to expand your knowledge through courses they offer or sponsor, or by paying your tuition. Sometimes courses are offered or sponsored by unions. Try to take advantage of those opportunities that interest you.

Look Your Best

When you are on the job, you will not only be dealing with the people around you, but you will also be representing your organization to the public. This means that you need to look your best *as appropriate to your job.* That last phrase is really the key.

Many suggestions about good grooming were given in the chapter on interviewing. Once you get the job, it would be a good idea to look those over again. Clean teeth, hair, nails, and body are a first essential. Of course, you may be on a job where you get dirty during the course of the day. Whether that is the case or not, a daily bath or shower are essential parts of good hygiene. Let's face it—it is very difficult to work with someone who has bad breath or who has a body odor from an unwashed body or unlaundered clothes. This may seem less important as a success skill to you than the others, but it is one that many employers mentioned in the studies.

Your choice of clothes should be governed by the kind of work you do. Look around at how others in your company and industry dress, and try to dress similarly, exercising your own taste at the same time. In general, the more conservative industries, like banking and law, require more conservative dress. Some industries require that you wear uniforms. In still others, you have more freedom of choice.

In any case, be sure your clothes fit you well and are kept clean. Avoid wearing party clothes or very casual clothes like shorts to work unless you are in a business where such clothing is called for. Remember the key word is *appropriate*.

Control Your Emotions

While you are on the job, many stresses and frustrations can occur that will test your ability to control your emotions. It is difficult to say just how much expression one is allowed on the job because of the many different situations that can arise.

Of course, physical fighting is not only forbidden but can land you in jail with a charge of assault or battery. Hollering and screaming, no matter how angry you get, are also not desirable on-the-job behaviors, although you will see some people shout. Crying, except in the most trying circumstances, usually just embarrasses everyone around you.

It is important that you find ways to communicate with your supervisor and your co-workers that are effective and that do not escalate your emotions to the point of a loss of control. Talking things through before they get too bad works well in some circumstances. Sometimes, however, you have to wait until you or the other person cools off. Each situation must be judged on its own.

Since most jobs come with some stress, it is a good idea to have some ways of reducing its effect on you. Some people find that regular physical activity helps. They walk or jog regularly or belong to a gym or team. Some people practice meditation or relaxation techniques. Other people like to read, listen to music, or pursue a hobby. Now that you have your first full-time job, if you do not have some ways of decompressing and reducing your tensions, try to find them.

Situation Study 6

Remember Carrie and Leonard from the previous situation study? Things have not improved in that office.

Neither of them was fired as a result of the first situation. A few weeks later, Leonard had to complete his quarterly sales report, which had a lot of figures. He completed it and gave it to Carrie to type. When it was finished, he submitted it to Ellen, their boss.

When Ellen read it, it didn't make much sense. The sales, which should have totaled the same when added up by customer and added up by week, did not do so. She called Leonard in and asked him to look at the report and figure out what was wrong.

Leonard took the report back to his desk and took out the information he had in his files. Somehow in typing, two columns of numbers had gotten jumbled.

He went back to Ellen. "Well," he said, "this is all Carrie's fault. Look, she typed these two columns wrong."

Ellen said, "I'm glad it's not a big mistake, but I want you to know that I hold you responsible. Although Carrie typed it, it's your report and you have to be sure it's correct before you give it to me. Please correct it and have it retyped for tomorrow."

Ellen left the office for a meeting. On her way back, while still in the hall, she could hear a loud voice coming from the office. She walked in to see Leonard standing next to Carrie, who was at her desk.

He was shouting, "What is wrong with you? Are you an idiot? Or did you do this to me on purpose? You never liked me. I'm going to get even for this. Now, you type this and you'd better get it right!"

Imagine you are Leonard Anderson.

How do you feel?

_____

_____

_____

_____

_____

_____

_____

What will you do?

_____

_____

_____

_____

_____

_____

_____

Imagine you are Carrie Curran.

How do you feel?

_____
_____
_____
_____
_____
_____
_____

What will you do?

_____
_____
_____
_____
_____
_____
_____

Imagine you are Ellen Brock.

How do you feel?

_____
_____
_____
_____
_____
_____
_____

What will you do?

_____
_____
_____
_____
_____
_____
_____

Become a Part of the Organization

Becoming a part of the organization is the last skill for success discussed because it is the most difficult one to explain. Daniel Goleman, a psychologist who has written extensively on how people get along in all kinds of organizations, says that people have to learn "what to say, what not to say, and what to call it."

If you think about your family for a few minutes, you may be able to understand what he means. Are there words you are not allowed to use in front of your parents or grandparents even though everyone knows those words? Are there things that have happened to family members that no one speaks about?

The same is true in the "family," or culture, of each organization. There are certain things that are done, other things that are not done, things that are said, and other things that are not said. As you become more experienced in work, you will find it easier to figure these out in each new organization you work for.

In the second skill for success related to getting along with your boss, the idea of adaptability was mentioned. You thought about needing to learn if your boss likes to structure everything you do or if he or she wants you to do more things on your own. That adaptability is an aspect of becoming part of the organization.

Michael Faber was hired for the data processing division of a large organization. He was a beginning worker with a lot of varied tasks. One day, Dawn Hays, his boss, asked him to look over a program that wasn't working to see if he could find the problem.

After a few hours of work, Michael called his boss over and said, "I found the problem. You made a mistake here."

Dawn bristled. "What do you mean *I* made a mistake?"

Michael pointed to the line of the program that had been written incorrectly and said, "Here it is."

"Oh," Dawn said, "fix it," and walked away angrily.

Michael had figured out what to say, but not what to call it. The answer to the question of what was wrong with the program was not *who* had made the error, particularly if that person was the boss, but *what* the error was. Michael should have said something like, "The problem is in line 46. A comma was needed instead of a space."

Knowing what to talk about at work and how to talk about it is a skill everyone learns. Of course, this can be carried too far. If you learn that the people or organization for which you are working are doing something that is illegal or unethical, then you are *not* supposed to keep quiet about it. Even if revealing the circumstances means that you will lose this particular job, in the long run you are definitely the winner.

Summary Worksheet

This chapter helped you understand ten skills for success drawn from research about what employers want.

The ten skills give a picture of the ideal employee. Your job is to identify the skills you already have and build upon them and to examine the skills where you are weaker so that you can strengthen your chances for success. Remember as you approach this, however, that nobody is perfect.

Put a check next to each skill you think you already have and a question mark next to those you want to work on.

_____ 1. I am dependable.

_____ 2. I know how to work well with my supervisor.

_____ 3. I know when to ask questions and when not to.

_____ 4. I can work cooperatively with my co-workers.

_____ 5. I carry out my responsibilities.

_____ 6. I take pride in what I do.

_____ 7. I have initiative. I like to learn new skills and take on new tasks.

_____ 8. I look my best on the job.

_____ 9. I can control my emotions on the job, and I have learned some ways of dealing with stress away from work.

_____ 10. I understand what it means to become a part of the organization.

CAREER
CHANGES | Section III

Moving Up 7

This section of the book is for the future. The first two sections concentrated on getting and keeping your first job. However, the chances are that you will not want things to stay the same forever. If all goes well, you will look for a raise, a promotion, or a new opportunity. Sometimes, in spite of our best efforts, life does not go as planned. Businesses close or particular positions are eliminated. Sometimes circumstance makes us change.

There are two chapters in this section of the book. This chapter is about opportunities within your current organization. It is about getting a raise on your first job and looking for a promotion within the same company. The next chapter takes you outside your current organization.

Getting a Raise

In the last chapter, you identified and learned how to apply ten skills for success. You are probably in line for a raise if you have worked on all these areas and your company or organization gives raises based on merit.

In some organizations, raises are based solely on length of employment. Each year you are there you get a specified salary raise, up to a certain point. This is true of many civil service jobs. In addition, for many civil service jobs the first period of employment (anywhere from six months to three years, depending on the job) is considered a probationary period. In the probationary period, you can be let go without the same kind of hearing and rights that you would have once you become a permanent employee. Your goal, if you want to remain on the job, is to become a permanent employee. If the job you hold is included in a collective bargaining agreement, then the salary increments each year are determined through negotiations between the union and your employer.

In some cases, there is a combination of a union scale and merit pay. Everyone gets at least the basic salary for the job and the number of years employed, but there is an opportunity to add merit pay. In general, it is the supervisor who puts in the request for merit pay for an employee.

If you are in an organization that does not have a standard salary schedule, there may still be a set period of review. Usually this review comes once a year. During the review period, you will discuss your accomplishments of the past year and your goals for work for the coming year. This is the point at which you can ask for a raise.

In some companies, there is no set pattern for salaries. Each person is on his or her own. It is appropriate to wait about a year after you are hired before asking for a raise. When you ask for a raise, the request should be based on your work and accomplishments. Do not talk about your financial need or obligations. You might also do some homework ahead of time to try and find out what raises people who are in jobs similar to yours have gotten. This will give you a clue as to what to expect, or if you are asked, to tell what you want.

Before you ask for a raise, you need to think about your accomplishments in the past year. To help you do that, complete the Raise Request Worksheet that follows. When you go in for that raise, be sure you remember your answers to the worksheet questions. Use them in your request.

Raise Request Worksheet

1. What new responsibilities have you taken on since you were hired?

_____

_____

_____

_____

2. What new skills have you acquired that you are now using on the job?

_____

_____

_____

_____

3. What special projects or activities were you involved in?

_____

_____

_____

_____

4. How did your work contribute to the product or service of the organization?

_____

_____

_____

_____

5. What praise or positive feedback have you received from your supervisor or others in the organization?

_____

_____

_____

_____

Getting Promoted

Perhaps you want more than a raise. A year or two have passed, and you have been getting signals from your supervisor and others within the organization that there may be an opening higher up for you.

To be sure that you are ready to take advantage of any opening, you need to know your organization. Some companies have *career ladders*. A career ladder is a path that many people are expected to take. There are, however, fewer and fewer positions as the rungs get higher. An example of a career ladder could be moving from typist in the pool, to secretary for a middle management executive, to office manager. Another career ladder is from sales clerk, to department manager, to a position in the management of the company as a whole.

If you are working for a large company, the personnel department or human resources department may have someone similar to a career counselor who is there to help you make your next moves within the organization. Keep in mind that, unlike a career counselor in school, this person is not very interested in helping you move *outside* the organization. You can ask if your organization has such a person or department, or you can watch for evidence of it. Usually if there is an active personnel department, you will see notices of jobs on bulletin boards or in company newsletters.

In addition to providing information on career opportunities, many companies will help you pay for additional education. Usually the courses you take or the degree you seek must be related to what you are doing and to the work of the company. If you have not completed college, you may be able to do so with a major in accounting or marketing or some other area of study useful to the company. If you have completed college, you may be able to take graduate level courses.

In some companies, the reimbursement is related to your grade in the course. An A will get you 100 percent reimbursement; a B, 75 percent; and so on. Again, you need to be observant and seek the information you want. You may have gotten a benefits booklet from the company and/or from a union when you were hired. Go back to that information now that you are ready for it.

The need for continuing education and training, whether paid for by your company or you, cannot be stressed enough. In 1986, the National Alliance of Business assessed the changes taking place in our society today to make some predictions. In the publication *Employment Policies: Looking to the Year 2000* they wrote:

There will be fewer natural career ladders. The
new technology makes it increasingly feasible
to separate "back office" functions (clerical,
service workers) from "front office" (technical,
sales, professional, management). It will thus
become more difficult to work up the ranks
through informal on-the-job training. More for-
malized training may be necessary.

In smaller organizations, the next step may not be
clearly laid out for you. The best thing to do is to talk
with your supervisor about what you might expect to do
and how to prepare for it. By keeping your eyes open, you
may see opportunities.

If you want to move up in your company, you will need
to find out the procedures that are followed. These may
include completing applications or presenting resumes.
There may be interviews just as for your first job. Look
over the information in chapters 3 and 4 on "papers" and
"people" to refresh your memory about these matters.
Also look ahead at the next section of this chapter, which
gives you some advice on applications, resumes, and interviews to use after you have had the experience of your
first full-time, paid job.

In the Promotions Opportunity Worksheet that follows, there are some questions you can use to assess the
opportunities for you in the company where you are now
working.

Promotions Opportunity Worksheet

1. Is there a personnel department within my organization?

_____

2. Does it provide any help on promotions?

_____

3. Is there a bulletin board where I work that shows opportunities for promotion?

_____

4. Is there a company or union newsletter that shows opportunities for promotion?

_____

5. Here are some opportunities that interest me:

a. _____

b. _____

c. _____

6. For which of those opportunities am I qualified?

_____

7. What can I do to improve my qualifications?

_____

_____

_____

_____

8. What help can I get from the company with my education?

_____

_____

_____

_____

9. What procedures do I follow to get the promotion I want?

_____

_____

_____

_____

Summary Worksheet

This chapter helped you examine ways you can move ahead within your own organization. Use the checklist that follows to be sure you understand how to be successful in asking for a raise or seeking a promotion.

_____I know my company policy on raises.

_____I know why I deserve a raise.

_____I can document the contributions that have earned me the right to ask for a raise.

_____I have examined the right time to ask for a raise.

_____I have planned how and when I will ask for a raise.

_____I know how to show that I am qualified for a promotion.

_____I have looked at the opportunities for promotion within my organization.

_____I know which jobs I am qualified for by my experience and education.

Moving Out

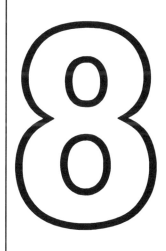

This chapter is about a bigger break—leaving the organization in which you held your first full-time job. The first section of the chapter reviews job-seeking skills. It adds some tips on how you can use the information about the experience you have gained in your new job search. You will see how to fill out applications, complete a resume, and answer interview questions. The last section of the book encourages you to find your own path.

Finding a New Job   If you have decided that there are no opportunities for the promotion you want within the organization where you are now working, it is time to move on. This means you have to take out and dust off the job-hunting skills and strategies that were discussed at the beginning of this book.

The second chapter of this book talked about how to

locate jobs. There is nothing new to add to your skills, but you have added a lot of people to those you knew before. While you may not want to advertise to everyone in your present organization that you are thinking about leaving, there may be some people you have met on the job or through the job who can help you. Add those people to your network. Then use all the resources you have—school placement offices, employment agencies, state employment services, newspaper ads, and networking.

The knowledge needed to fill out a job application will not change; nor will the need to be accurate, definite, honest, and complete; to read directions; and to complete the application neatly. You still need to think through your education and work histories and all your dates and places again. However, the information for your job application will change because you will now have a full-time, paid position to enter in the work history area.

Before you go to complete your first job application, think about how you can fill in your duties and responsibilities. You will have very little space to say all that you have done in the last year or two. Practice getting your description down to the fewest possible words.

In addition, you now have to answer the question, "Reason for Leaving," with something other than "Returned to school." It is important that you do *not* give a negative answer like, "Could not get along with my boss," or "Disliked my fellow workers," or "My boss was stupid." Surely there is some positive reason you are leaving, such as "Seeking a better paying position," or "Desire promotion with more responsibility."

Finally, you will probably have different references to give. Try to find references that are as business-related as possible. You usually cannot list your immediate supervisor because that person is already listed in your work history section. However, if you have had good relations with other supervisors in your organization or you have gotten to know clients or customers of the organization you have been with, you can list them. Be sure you consider whether the person you are listing knows you well enough to give you a good reference. Be sure to ask for permission in person, by telephone, or by mail before you list anyone.

In chapter 3, we saw the application of Sandra Yee, who had graduated from community college with an associate's degree in accounting and was looking for a job as a bookkeeper. Sandra got that job and continued in college to complete her bachelor's degree. Sandra's new application form is filled out on the pages that follow.

Sample Job Application Form

Date of Application _7-1-94_   Social Security No. _123-45-6789_

Full Name (Last, First) _YEE, SANDRA_

Address _6105 DAWN ROAD_

City _INDIANAPOLIS_   State _INDIANA_   Zip _46240_

Home Telephone _(317) 442-1010_   Business Telephone _(317) 474-1000_

Position Applied For _ACCOUNTANT_

Referred By _NEWSPAPER ADVERTISEMENT 6-30-94_

When will you be available to begin work? _TWO WEEKS AFTER HIRING_

Can you travel if the job requires it? _YES_

Have you been employed here before? _NO_   If Yes, Give Date _—_

Have you applied for a job here before? _NO_   If Yes, Give Date _—_

Are you a United States citizen? _YES_

If no, do you have an alien registration card and will you produce it for inspection? _—_

If you are a veteran of the U. S. Military Service, give dates of service and branch. _NA_

Have you been convicted of a crime in the last seven years? _NO_

If Yes, Give Date _—_   Place _—_   Offense _—_

Education:	Name and Address of School	No. of Years Attended	Did you Graduate	Major/Degree
High School	RIPPLE HS 855 E 59 INDIANAPOLIS	4	YES	ACADEMIC
College	INDIANA UNIVERSITY 900 W. NEW YORK ST INDIANAPOLIS	3	YES	ACCOUNTING
Trade School or Other	INDIANAPOLIS COMMUNITY COLLEGE 7331 STATION ST.	2	YES	ACCOUNTING

Special Training

Employment History (Start with your most recent position)

Name & Address of Employer or Organization	Dates Employed From Month/Year To Month/Year	Nature of Work	Reason for Leaving	Name of Supervisor	Salary
GENERAL SUPPLIES 3000 E 48 ST INDIANAPOLIS	7/92 - PRESENT	FULL CHARGE BOOKKEEPER	SEEKING ADVANCE- MENT	MARVIN BROWN	$18,000
CORN + MORE SUPERMARKET 420 W. NEW YORK ST. INDIANAPOLIS	9/90 - 5/92	BOOKKEEPER	TOOK FULL-TIME JOB	NEAL MCKINLAY	$5.00 PER HOUR
NA					
NA					

References (Other than supervisors listed above)

Name	Full Address	Telephone	Relationship
LINDA CAREY	CORN+MORE SUPERMARKET 420 W. NEW YORK ST INDIANAPOLIS	275- 1000	OWNER OF STORE
DUANE SMITH	DEPARTMENT OF ACCOUNTING INDIANA UNIVERSITY 900 W. NEW YORK ST	311- 4118	PROFESSOR
CAROL RICHMOND	DEPARTMENT OF MATHEMATICS INDIANA UNIVERSITY 900 W NEW YORK ST	311- 4125	PROFESSOR

Special Skills (foreign languages, licenses, association memberships)

FAMILIAR WITH IBM PC AND USE OF SPREADSHEETS

If you have ever been known by any other name, please indicate.

NA

Just as you may have needed a resume for your first job, you may need one now. Review the five steps to a winning resume explained in detail in chapter 3. If you want more information, use the book *How to Write a Winning Résumé* (VGM Career Horizons).

Five steps to a winning resume—a brief review

1. Examine the relevant areas of your life in depth.

2. Translate the details into action words and the vocabulary of work.

3. Write a rough draft of the resume.

4. Arrange your resume on the page so that it is easy to read and attractive.

5. Proofread your resume.

Just as with the application, there is no change in the process. What changes is your content. You need to put more emphasis on your accomplishments in your full-time, paid job and less on school activities and other accomplishments.

In chapter 3, we saw the resume of Philip Juarez, who was looking for a job as an assistant to a buyer after he graduated from high school. He got the job and is now ready to move on. His resume after two years of experience is on the following page. Compare his two resumes. Then begin work on your resume. Remember that you will also need a cover letter to accompany the resume whenever you mail it.

Sample Resume—with Two Years of Work

Philip Juarez
571 Vermont Street
Brooklyn, New York 11207
(718) 555-3450

EDUCATION

Albert Einstein High School, Diploma, June 1990
Major: Merchandising
Specialized Courses: Retailing, Fashion Communications, Data Processing, Junior Achievement
                       Economics, Art Electives in Display and Package Design
Extracurricular Activities: School boutique purchase and sales committees

WORK EXPERIENCE

1990–1992   ASSISTANT TO THE BUYER   Ajax Merchandising Consortium
               CHILDREN'S WEAR   New York, New York

Assisted in all aspects of purchasing of children's wear. Accompanied buyer to showrooms and participated in decision making. Carried out follow-up of orders by telephone and letters. Kept records of orders from retailers on an IBM PC. Worked with computer consultant to establish record keeping system that would track orders filled, orders to be filled, and merchandise available from wholesalers.

1989–1990   STOCK CLERK   Blooms Department Store
                                           New York, New York

Stocked shelves, monitored supplies on the floor. Took inventory. Assisted in unpacking and packing. (Part-time work while in school.)

Summer 1988   MAINTENANCE WORKER   Parks Department
                                           New York, New York

Participated in all indoor and outdoor cleanup activities in various parts of Central Park.

SKILLS

Familiar with the IBM PC and several data processing and word processing software packages.

Type 60 WPM.

You also have to prepare for job interviews as you did before. Look over chapter 4 on interviewing. You will need to prepare yourself now as you did then. You were successful in getting your first job. The second one is usually easier to get. Now you have that thing that all employers say they want: *experience!*

It is your job to translate that experience into terms that will sound appealing to your next employer. He or she wants to be sure you are bringing something valuable that you gained on your last job and that you are not leaving because you failed. Employers like to see experience because they can use how you performed on your previous job to predict how you will do on your next job. Of course, unless you are going to work for someone who saw you at work, most of what they know will come from you.

Be prepared to answer questions about the job you have now—the one you are leaving. You can expect a question about why you want to change jobs. Avoid being overly critical of your previous boss or company. It makes the new employer worry that you will also be overly critical of her or him. Focus on your positive reasons for leaving. Do you want a job with more room for growth? Do you want a job with more responsibility and the higher rewards that go with it? Do you want to use the experiences you have had to meet new challenges?

Some other questions you may be asked that relate to your work are listed on the worksheet that follows:

Interview Questions About Your Job

1. What were your major experiences on your last job?

_____

_____

2. What did you learn on your last job that you can use here?

_____

_____

3. What was the biggest problem you faced on your last job?

_____

_____

4. How did you solve that problem?

_____

_____

5. What did you like best about your last job?

_____

_____

6. What did you like least about it?

_____

_____

7. What was your most rewarding experience at work?

_____

_____

Use the same principles and worksheets that you used to prepare for your first set of job interviews. You will find them in chapter 4. There are more of them in the book *How to Have a Winning Job Interview* (VGM Career Horizons).

In addition, use the worksheet that follows to match your experience in your first job with the skills needed in your new job.

Job-to-Job Worksheet

Current Job Responsibilities   **Skill Acquired**   **New Job Responsibilities**

Example: Prepared showroom   Arrangement of products   Window arrangements
display

On Your Own

This book has presented a number of ways of getting—and keeping—your first job. However, no matter how many different examples we give, life itself can be more complicated. For example, in the chapter on career ladders, there was no discussion of the kind of person who jumps ahead quickly, skipping many steps and going from the mailroom to the president's office in a couple of quick leaps. Yet these things happen.

The best way to use this book is to decide what you want to do at any current stage in your life and then use the sections that apply. Not everyone wants to follow the same path. A very good book about making your own path is *How to Not Make It. . . and Succeed* by Anna Miller-Tiedeman (LIFECAREER® Foundation).

You may want to work for a while and then stop and go to school, or you may want to work for someone else and then try a business of your own. You may see some way the organization you are working for can really do better and decide to sell that idea, breaking all the rules of who speaks to whom. Remember, you can do whatever you decide to do.

Perhaps instead of looking for promotions or raises, you would like to think about working for yourself, running your own business. There are many books about running each different kind of business. A good general book to begin with is *Working for Yourself,* produced by the National Career Information System.

A few last words—do not be in too much of a hurry by *always* thinking about how to get ahead. If every step in life is just to prepare you for the next step, when do you get to enjoy the step you are on?

Summary Worksheet

Look back over this chapter to be sure you know how to make the most of your experience when you begin to think about getting a new job. Use the checklist to be sure you have left nothing out.

_____ I know how to go about finding a new job.

_____ I have reviewed the information about job applications, and I have prepared a new worksheet with current information.

_____ I have identified new references.

_____ I have gone over the methods for writing a resume, and I have written a new one.

_____ I have prepared a new sample cover letter.

_____ I have prepared myself for an interview. I am ready to talk about how my experiences on my present job prepare me for my new job.

_____ I have thought about my personal career direction and realize there are many alternatives open to me.

_____ I am enjoying my career.

Related Readings

Books to Help You in Your Job Search

The Civil Service Administrative Handbook. ARCO, New York: 1988.

Creative Visualization. Shakti Gawain, Bantam Books, New York: 1979.

How to Choose the Right Career. Louise Welsh Schrank, VGM Career Horizons, Lincolnwood, Illinois: 1991.

How to Have a Winning Job Interview. Deborah Perlmutter Bloch, VGM Career Horizons, Lincolnwood, Illinois: 1992.

How to Make the Right Career Moves, Deborah Perlmutter Bloch, VGM Career Horizons, Lincolnwood, Illinois: 1990.

How to Not Make It...and Succeed. Anna Miller-Tiedeman, LIFECAREER® Foundation, Los Angeles: 1987.

How to Write a Winning Resume. Deborah Perlmutter Bloch, VGM Career Horizons, Lincolnwood, Illinois: 1990.

Occupational Outlook Handbook, U.S. Department of Labor, VGM Career Horizons, Lincolnwood, Illinois: 1992-93 edition.

Opportunities in Insurance Careers. Robert Schrayer, VGM Career Horizons, Lincolnwood, Illinois: 1987. (There are many other books in this series covering individual careers such as *Opportunities in High Tech Careers, Opportunities in Military Careers,* and *Opportunities in Carpentry Careers.*)

The Seven Habits of Highly Effective People, Stephen R. Covey, Simon and Schuster, New York: 1989.

What Color is Your Parachute? Richard Nelson Bolles, Ten Speed Press, Berkeley, California: 1992.

Working for Yourself. National Career Information System, Eugene, Oregon: 1988.

Selected Reserch on Employability Skills

Business Criteria for Entry Level Office Employee Competencies. W. Alwell and W. Daggett, New York State Education Department, Albany: 1977.

Employability: Review and Survey. John Hartz et al., the Vocational Studies Center, University of Wisconsin, Madison: 1978.

"Employer Measures of Industry Satisfaction" in *System-Wide Tests of Occupational Programs.* Deborah Perlmutter (Bloch), New York City Board of Education, Brooklyn: 1982. (Also Eric Document ED 218 474.)

Employers' Views on Hiring and Training. Edith F. Lynton, Joel R. Seldin, and Sara Gruhin, Labor Market Information Network, New York: 1978, 1979, 1981.

Employment Policies: Looking to the Year 2000. National Alliance of Business, 1986.

National Career Development Guidelines. National Occupational Information Coordinating Committee, Washington, D.C.: 1989.

Pilot-Study to Determine the Need for Curriculum Modification in Vocational-Technical Education. W. Annis and J. Perrigo, New Hampshire State Department of Education, Concord, New Hampshire: 1968.

What Work Requires of Schools: A SCANS Report for America 2000. U.S. Department of Labor, Government Printing Office, Washington, D.C.: 1991.

VGM CAREER BOOKS

VGM Career Horizons
a division of *NTC Publishing Group*
4255 West Touhy Avenue
Lincolnwood, Illinois 60646-1975